The Canadian Garden Primer

AN ORGANIC APPROACH

MARK CULLEN

ACKNOWLEDGEMENTS

I cannot take credit for the contents in this book. But I will take responsibility for it.

This is easy to do, when you work with a team that is thorough, thoughtful in their work and professional in every way.

Let us just say that it would not exist if it were up to me to follow through on the countless details that a book of this magnitude requires. It has been, after all, a 3 year project!

At the top of the list is my assistant Brenda Hensley. Wow. You have no idea how many times I have asked her, "What is next?" "Where did that go?" and "Would you mind following up with…." Her answers to these and many other questions are always right on the mark. Suffice it to say that once this book is off the press, Brenda deserves a very nice vacation.

To my professional editor Karen York, humble thanks. Humble: because you know the craft of word-smithing so well and I always learn so much from you.
Thanks because there is no other word that fits.

To graphic designer Susan Robinson. One of the great talents in the business. I had the pleasure of working with Susan for almost 26 years while I was in the retail gardening business. It has been great to get back together and feel the same rush that comes when a creative project like this takes shape.

To my friends at Home Hardware – and I do not use the term 'friends' lightly! Ray Gabel, Joel Marks and Derril Linseman among many others have been very supportive of this 'project'. Thanks for your commitment to the Canadian Garden Primer and for cheering Brenda and I along!

To daughter Emma: a business student at Dalhousie who moonlights as a photographer. She is good! You saved us from some tight spots too kid! Love you.

To my wife Mary and our other 3 kids – Lynn, Heather and Ben, many thanks for being there, even when I am not (travel takes me away from home all too often). Your support of my work means more to me than you know. Often you provide inspiration to me at the most surprising of times!

| DEDICATION |

"To my Aunt Charlotte and Tom [Lawrence] Cullen"
Great gardening inspirations, at 90 years old.

"Work too hard and you are looking for trouble.
Don't work hard enough and trouble will come looking for you"

Joseph Genova, my barber.

A portion of the proceeds from the sale of each book
will be donated to S.H.A.R.E. Agricultural Foundation.
A Hand Up not a Hand Out!
Check out their great work at www.shareagfoundation.org

Copyright MaryMarkCommunications Inc., 2008

Published by MaryMark Communications Inc.

MaryMark Communications, 136 Main Street, Unionville, Ontario, Canada L3R 2G5

Mark Cullen
www.markcullen.com

Although all reasonable care has been taken in the preparation of this book, neither the publisher nor the author can accept responsibility for any consequences arising from the use thereof or from the information contained within.

National Library of Canada Cataloguing in Publication Data

Cullen, Mark, 1956-
    The Canadian garden primer, an organic approach

Includes index

ISBN 978-0-9782665-2-3

First printing 2008

Book Designed & Produced by Firefly Studios, www.firefly-studios.ca

Printed and Bound in Canada

CONTENTS

INTRODUCTION

Welcome to the New World of Gardening.

Think about it - a generation from now, people will reflect on how things have changed in Canadian gardens, and how Canadian gardeners themselves have changed. Times change, so do we.

It still seems like yesterday when my dad, Len Cullen, introduced me to the "movers and shakers" of the Canadian gardening business. In the summer of 1976, we traveled across Ontario and out to British Columbia in search of a new crop of nursery stock with which to feed the demand for quality plant material the following spring at Weall and Cullen, our retail gardening enterprise in Toronto.

During those weeks in cars and planes, we talked about the nature of Canadian gardeners. Dad was a quiet and private man but needed little coaxing to reflect aloud on the many changes that he had seen in his 30 or so years in the business.

In the early 1940s, he was a teenager, about a year too young to go to war in Europe, and his mentor and friend John Weall was in his middle age, a British veteran of the First World War. In spite of their age difference, they were the best of friends. In fact, young Len Cullen was somewhat of a surrogate son to John, who never had a son of his own.

Dad remembered how in 1943 they grew perennials on a small property on Lake Simcoe (where they could afford land, far from the inflated real estate values of Toronto). On their two acres they grew only as many daylilies (or *Hemerocallis* as John would insist they be called), peonies, astilbes, rock cress and many other herbaceous perennials that they could reasonably keep hoed and weed-free.

Each spring, they would travel to the lake to divide and replant their crop. The divisions were for John's customers back in the city and the remaining roots were replanted for future weeding and nurturing for later division.

The gardening business seemed so simple then. You would visit a client who needed some help designing a garden and, sitting in their kitchen, you sketched something on a piece of graph paper. The choice of plant material was rather limited as all of it was grown within a short driving distance and was available only in early spring.

Nursery stock was shipped or picked up from the farm while the plants were dormant - a six-week window from about the third week of April to the end of May, in a good year. This was also the time when they planted all but the large trees and evergreens that were prepared for sale in the field by digging the root ball and wrapping burlap around it, hence "balled and burlapped."

By the late 1970s, however, things had changed a lot indeed. The age of containerized nursery stock had dawned. Field-grown perennials did not exist, except perhaps on the smallest of wholesale farms. All the perennials purchased at retail were grown in containers, while trees, shrubs and evergreens were, for the most part, grown in pots or dug using a mechanical 'tree spade' and 'planted' into wire baskets.

Things have continued to change. When I wrote my first hardcover gardening book, *The Greener Thumb*, in 1990, there was no GST and virtually no competition for a "complete guide to Canadian gardening." "Organic" was a concept embraced by a small group of hippie-wanna-bes. The top-selling plants at most garden centres were junipers (hardly the case now). And pretty much the only place that most Canadians could go for a selection of plants and reliable gardening advice was an independent garden centre.

Here we are a decade into the new millennium and the whole idea of the new millennium is no longer new. In fact, my kids refer to it as the "turn of the century" so we middle-aged folk are forced to refer to the early 1900's as the "turn of the *last* century."

My book, *The Greener Thumb*, was to a new generation of gardeners what I hope this book, *The Canadian Garden Primer*, will be to another. Here, I celebrate the new Canadian gardener and her/his garden. Woven into each page is an approach to gardening that is now being embraced by vast numbers - we refer to it loosely as "organic." In essence, this means treating the soil as the life support system of garden plants and therefore refraining from using synthetic chemicals. The organic gardener doesn't have to worry about poisoning either soil or water, and children and pets can play freely in our yards with no concern about contacting toxic substances.

Today, this is mainstream stuff.

In the 1950s, John Weall said that the weed killer 2,4-D changed gardening more than any other thing. I would suggest that the demise of its use over recent years has changed things even more.

No longer obsessed with eliminating weeds from our lawns, we have found environmentally responsible ways of growing and managing our "living carpets of green."

We have changed, the ways we garden have changed and, most importantly, our vision of a beautiful garden has changed. Today, the snapshot of the dream garden can be just as easily one of vegetables and herbs, fruiting trees and berry bushes as a traditional English garden. It often is a mixture of the two - food plants and ornamentals growing together in a canvas of beauty.

For that matter, the new Canadian gardener's perfect garden is not exclusively a garden at all, but a place where we entertain, rest, read, listen to an electronic device of some kind or simply drink in the delightful sound of birdsong and moving water.

This book is a celebration of that place.

The Canadian Garden Primer provides you with the basic information that you will need to make all sorts of plants work successfully in the overall scheme that we still call a garden. Woven into this information are stories that I have heard from other Canadian gardeners plus reflections of my own, of course.

If you engage yourself in the experience of gardening - both the physical activity and the multi-sensory experience of just being in the garden - you will have your own stories.

Our lives seem to be increasingly taken over by high technology, and our time ever more consumed with sedentary indoor activities. But I predict that our desire to be a part of the birdsong and natural fragrances that we associate with the garden will not change, only the intensity of our desire to enjoy them. Time may change us, but we will forever want to escape to the garden - an escape not from reality but *to* reality, as my friend Karen York likes to say.

If this edition finds a privileged place on your bookshelf or the coffee table, I truly hope that you pick it up often to reference a particular question that you have about Canadian gardening. And I hope that you stay for a good read and inspiration.

Keep your knees dirty,

Mark Cullen

P.S. This is the age of interaction - when reader and writer can communicate freely via the internet. I would love to hear your gardening stories and reflections.

Contact me at www.markcullen.com.

MarkCullen.com

PART ONE
The Non-Edible Garden

Successful gardeners spend a lot of time matchmaking. This has less to do with putting romance in the garden than taking the lot that has been handed you and matching it to the most desirable plants.

It's critical to have a vision of what you want your garden to look like, as well as an understanding of your soil conditions and exposure (sun/shade) so you can select plants that will be happy in your particular site.

I advise you to get advice on both scores. A professional garden designer or landscape architect will help you to put an image of the gorgeous garden that you have in your head onto paper (or, more accurately, a computer screen). He or she will ask you pertinent questions that you might not have thought of to create a garden suited to you specifically.

BEFORE YOU CALL THE PROFESSIONALS!
Your garden should be functional (that is, meet *your* needs for the space), pleasing to the eye and be a place where you can spend your free time. It shouldn't take more time than you have available to maintain it. If you have little time to spend gardening, choose low maintenance, slow-growing plants. If you love to garden and intend to spend your leisure hours tending your landscape, you have a wider variety in terms of design and landscape plants from which to choose.

Professional designers deal with the fundamental shape of your garden, including hardscaping such as patios, pathways and decks, the placement of major trees and shrubs, and the allotment

As the Shasta daisies finish in my garden, the black-eyed Susans begin their show.

START WITH A PLAN
Whether you are planning an urban, suburban or rural garden, starting out with a well-thought-out garden plan is a fine idea because:

- *Time spent on a garden plan in the beginning will save hours of work in the long run.*

- *A plan addresses your specific needs and gives the best results for years to come.*

- *It will save you money: it minimizes the potential for costly mistakes.*

- *It makes optimum use of the plants; there's little point waiting for a favourite tree to grow if it is poorly situated on your lot.*

of space for things such as a children's play area, shed, vegetable garden, pond, etc. Good garden designers will recommend particular plants once they understand your needs relative to your lifestyle, family members (children, pets), etc. Their recommendations of colour schemes are generally limited to the foliage colour and contrast of permanent plants and flowering shrubs. Planning for annual colour is left up to you.

Each plant species has preferences and most plants will adapt to a range of soil conditions if their light requirements are met. The sales people at your local garden centre have a wealth of knowledge and can help you select plants that are best suited to your garden.

Colourful petunias "punch up" an otherwise ordinary garden.

CHAPTER ONE
The Sun-Loving Garden

Usually facing south or west, a full-sun garden generally receives sunlight all day long, including the most intense afternoon sun. With these conditions, you have optimum growing conditions for many flowering plants, trees and shrubs, and *the greatest number of plants to choose from*. Your biggest challenge lies not in finding plants that will grow in your sunny garden, but choosing from the almost limitless possibilities!

Of course, full sun may create quite different conditions depending on where you are in Canada. The long summer days and intense heat of the Canadian Prairies can actually burn a so-called sun-loving plant, while the same plant on the West or East Coast may perform very well in a sunny garden.

I define a sunny garden as one that receives six hours or more of sun per day and where the prevailing weather for the gardening season is sunny-not cloudy. Such conditions are easily met on the Prairies. More difficult are areas in the eastern Maritimes (generally, the closer to the Atlantic Ocean you go, the greater the number of cloudy days) and on the west side of the Rocky Mountains.

CHOOSING THE RIGHT PLANTS
When choosing which plants to use in the sun, consider carefully: *size, colour, bloom time, texture, scent, the ability to attract birds and insects, drought-tolerance and hardiness.*

Nursery tags list much of this information, including a number indicating a plant's hardiness zone. These zones, going from 0 to 8 in Canada, are determined by average winter temperatures, 0 being the coldest and 8 the warmest. For example, a plant that is hardy to Zone 3 should survive average winter temperatures as low as -40° to -34°C. If you are a new gardener, I advise you to become familiar with the growing zone that you live in. Take a look at the map on page 200 for more information. To be more certain of success, choose plants with a lower number than your zone.

That said, there are other factors that influence a plant's survival, such as wind, soil conditions and snow cover. Remember that snow is the best free plant insulation that you can find! It protects the roots of plants from severe temperatures and the freeze-and-thaw-cycles that are so common during Canadian winters. A Zone 6 plant might survive in Zone 5 given good snow cover, but die without it.

Complicating the matter is that the United States has a different hardiness zone system, with 11 zones (0 to 10), and many plants offered for sale in Canada include an American-made plant tag—often with "inaccurate" information.

While checking a tag, always look for the plant's mature size. It is important to envision how a garden will look not only when first planted, but also in five and 10 years' time. Rather than trying to control the size of a plant by continual pruning, choose plants whose ultimate size is suited to their location in the garden.

The other day, I received a call on my radio show from a frustrated listener. He had planted a silver lace vine (*Polygonum aubertii*) on a chain link fence next to a mature apple tree. The vine had grown to the top of the fence the first year and leapt from it to the apple tree in the second year. By the third year, it was growing through the top of the apple tree and wreaking havoc. He was worried that the tree was going to be choked by the vine. Little did he know that the vine was at risk of dying in another eight or 10 years (such is its nature). *I put silver lace vine in the category of plants that perform won-derfully for the person who is A): impatient and B): plans to move within five years.* So you really need to know that a plant is appropriate to your space before you buy it.

Also Keep in mind that the amount of sun your garden receives may change over time as plants mature. That lovely silver birch might make a nice focal point to your backyard now, but will it be casting shade over the flower beds in five years?

A mix of annuals, perennials and evergreens can create a beautiful garden.

Yellow Rudbeckia and purple Veronica mix well.

Another important consideration when choosing plants is bloom time—when they flower and for how long. The goal of most gardeners, whether working in sun or shade, is to create a garden with a succession of colour from spring through late fall. A good design not only guarantees a garden full of blooms all summer but also creates a wonderfully fluid, ever-changing palette of colours in the landscape. An inspired garden design will do all that in an ecological and esthetically pleasing way, as well as take into account how you want to use your outdoor space.

Flowering annual plants are known for their quick growth and extended bloom that can start in late spring and carry on into fall until frost kills them. Used on their own or to fill spaces among other plants, they can be successfully added to the garden for instant colour throughout the growing season.

Perennial plants return each year with specific, usually shorter, flowering times that can be coordinated to fill each season with colour. As a rule, perennials grow bigger each year, so the need for annuals as filler diminishes. This habit of perennials to outperform themselves from year to year requires judicious selection of variety and species. *To be blunt: if you choose poorly, you may have some explaining to do.*

In an extreme case of "perennial regret," my sister Sue, who lived in Pickering, Ontario, for some years, discovered the joy of growing ribbon grass (*Phalaris arundinacea*). As is her nature, i.e. generous, she divided her ribbon grass and gave it away to every neighbour she came into contact with. Why not—it grew nicely and she had lots! About five years passed before she realized that this wonderful plant is considered by many to be a weed—a good-looking weed, but a weed. Her answer to the problem? She moved. Which was probably a good idea as you really cannot kill ribbon grass.

ADVANTAGES AND CHALLENGES OF THE SUNNY GARDEN

Sunny gardens not only offer endless possibilities for a wide range of prolific flowering plants but can also produce an abundance of vegetables, herbs and fruit. Rock gardens and meadow gardens also have the greatest success in sunny sites.

However, full sun does make certain demands of the gardener. Many plants love the sun, but so do weeds, which have adapted to dry conditions and will compete with garden plants for water and nutrients. Planting densely will make it tough for weeds to establish themselves.

The heat of full sun causes both plants and soil to lose a great deal of moisture very quickly, so the gardener must both supplement and preserve Mother Nature's water supply. Choosing drought-tolerant plants-generally those with fuzzy, silver, succulent, spiny or needled leaves - is just one way of reducing water demands. (See Chapter 15 for more on ways to conserve water.)

A solid show of colour like this is the result of close planting and judicious weeding.

MULCH, MY FRIENDS, MULCH

I frequently talk about the benefits of mulch-and in a sunny garden, it can mean the difference between success and frustration. A layer five centimetres (two inches) thick of finely ground pine or cedar bark mulch helps to insulate the soil against extreme temperature fluctuations and dramatically reduces moisture loss from evaporation. It also suppresses weeds and eventually breaks down, adding nutrients to the soil. (See Chapter 16 for more on mulch. This is important! I call it my " mulch treatise".)

WATER WISELY

It is best to water early in the morning or in the evening to allow the moisture time to soak into the soil without evaporating. Watering at the soil level is more efficient than overhead sprinklers. Soaker hoses, which have a weeping action, reduce both evaporation loss and run-off. They are ideal for use in gardens, around trees and shrubs

Save water with Mark's Choice Soaker Hose.

KEY ELEMENT

WORK WITH NATURE

A principle of garden design—and cultivation generally—that I live by is this: look to nature for cues. Copy her in your garden and you'll create a garden that looks and feels consistent with the natural world around you. For instance, if you live in an area with many existing rocks, incorporate them into your landscape plan. On the other hand, large rocks introduced into idyllic farm country might seem an aberration. So don't fight nature...work with her. She knows better than we do, anyway.

---

and along walkways. Many soaker hoses, including my Mark's Choice hoses, use recycled rubber and are made right here in Canada. (See Chapter 15 for more on water conservation.)

MODERATING YOUR SUN

If you experience high-intensity sun in your garden, I suggest that you introduce a little afternoon shade. By filtering, not eliminating, the sun, especially during the hottest part of the day, you can reduce the stress on plants and make the garden a more

inviting place for you and your visitors to use and enjoy.

There are several options available for cooling outdoor spaces, ranging from permanent structures to planting trees and large shrubs. Building or planting to create shade in your yard is a great excuse to be creative and have some fun. Determine where your trees, plants or structures must be located to provide shade when you are most inclined to use your garden.

A pergola covered in a variety of vines introduces welcome shade into an otherwise sunny garden.
(UBC Botanical Garden)

A troublesome "hot spot" will be cooled down when you plant a shade tree.

A shade tree is the best solution if space permits. Planting a young shade tree now will bring increased shade to the yard with each growing season. Planted on the south side of your house, a shade tree will help keep it cool in summer and, once the tree drops its leaves, will allow the sun in to heat the house in winter. Or site it beside a patio or porch; nothing beats sitting there looking up into a leafy canopy.

Awnings and umbrellas can provide shade, too, and have the advantage of being moveable. More permanent structures such as arbours and pergolas are effective on their own but can be even better when planted with vines and shrubs to create a green, living shelter.

Annual vines such as morning glories or runner beans give you the flexibility of changing them from year to year. Because they die off with severe frost, there will be more sunlight reaching the yard in winter when we are craving UV rays. Perennial vines are in it for the long term and can offer shade, flowers, fruit, fall colour and often beautiful winter structure, too. Try to plant native species where possible (American bittersweet instead of Oriental bittersweet, for example). (See Chapter 6 for more on native plants.)

No, this is not my wisteria vine. If only!

ANNUAL CLIMBERS

- Black-eyed Susan vine
  (*Thunbergia alata*)

- Hyacinth bean
  (*Lablab purpureus*)

- Mandevilla
  (*Mandevilla* x *amoena*)

- Moonflower vine
  (*Ipomoea alba*)

- Morning glory
  (*Ipomoea purpurea*)

- Scarlet runner bean
  (*Phaseolus coccineus*)

- Sweet pea
  (*Lathyrus odoratus*)

Morning glory

'Improved Blaze' climbing rose, a long-standing favourite, is hardy to Zone 4 and produces a vivid show.

CLIMBING PERENNIALS FOR STRUCTURES

VARIETY	HARDINESS ZONE	VARIETY	HARDINESS ZONE
American bittersweet (*Celastrus scandens*)	2	Hardy kiwi vine (*Actinidia arguta*)	5
Boston ivy (*Parthenocissus tricuspidata*)	4	Hops (*Humulus lupulus*)	3
Clematis (*Clematis* spp.)	3	Trumpet honeysuckle (*Lonicera sempervirens*)	4
Climbing hydrangea (*Hydrangea anomala* ssp. *petiolaris*)	4	Trumpet vine (*Campsis radicans*)	5
Climbing roses (*Rosa* spp.)	4	Virginia creeper (*Parthenocissus quinquefolia*	2
Dutchman's pipe (*Aristolochia durior*)	5	Wisteria (*Wisteria*)	4

* See plant hardiness zone map on page 200 -201

Hosta.

CHAPTER TWO
The Shade-Loving Garden

I can't tell you how many times I have heard someone lament, "I can't garden, all I have is shade!" Wrong!

For 18 years, my wife Mary and I lived in the shade of a hardwood forest—the building lot was carved out of a sugar maple bush. True, for the first few years I struggled with the many plants that I planted there. By the fifth year, however, I hit my stride and began to see many of the perennials and shrubs in my garden scheme maturing into something very beautiful. Our shady garden was filled with a fabulous assortment of shrubs, bulbs, flowers and foliage. We could be outside comfortably reading in a chair or deadheading flowers even in the heat of the mid-afternoon. I discovered what many gardeners know—there are advantages to shade over full sun, despite some preconceived prejudices about it.

SHADY ADVANTAGES

The majority of weeds are adapted to the hot, dry, bright conditions of full sun, so shade gardens often have fewer problems with noxious invaders. Many pests also avoid the shade. Without the heat of full sun, gardens shaded by a structure lose less moisture to evaporation so their watering needs are reduced. The cooling effect of shade means that the soil holds on to moisture longer, allowing plants to access it throughout the day. Although shade trees also keep the air cooler and reduce evaporation, their roots can suck a lot of moisture out of the ground.

Slower rates of photosynthesis caused by the absence of sun mean that plants don't deplete soil nutrients as quickly so fertilizing can be reduced or even eliminated.

While some people assume that their plant choices are limited for a shade garden, experienced shade gardeners will tell you that there are all sorts of fabulous shade plants on the market.

Ferns thrive in shaded conditions.

And native plant enthusiasts will point out that the shade garden is the perfect setting for a native woodland garden. It is well worth the effort to choose shade-tolerant plants rather than struggle to grow plants not suited to these growing conditions.

Shade also protects you and your family from both the heat and the harmful UV radiation of the sun. It's no surprise that more people are asking for landscape designs that include structures such as pergolas to provide shade.

SHADE IS RELATIVE

It is important to keep in mind that shade is different at different times of the day. Generally, afternoon shade is better for plants than morning shade as it gives plants a respite from the harshest, hottest sun.

Morning shade is what I call "cool shade."

"A spot that is sunny in the morning receives the coolest sunshine of the day". By the time an eastern exposure heats up, it is mid- to late morning and soon to be in shadows for the afternoon. The east side of the house is the perfect place for plants that dehydrate quickly, like hydrangea and coleus. For this reason shade-loving plants often perform quite well on the east side of the house.

"The west side of a brick or stone wall tends to be very sunny and hot." The radiant heat that is absorbed by the wall is fine for true heat-seeking plants, but can be a difficult place to grow plants that do not thrive in bright sun.

While walls, buildings and fences cast permanent shade, you can also create temporary shade with plants. In a sunny border, for example, put in statuesque plants such as giant fleece-flower, Joe-Pye weed and maiden grasses, and you can safely plant shade-lovers in their shadow.

TYPES OF SHADE

You may find definitions of the different types of shade contradictory

and a bit baffling. Shade is usually divided into a number of categories, with the heaviest shade referred to as dense or deep shade. After that there is a host of shade descriptions: dappled, light, open, semi, thin, partial, medium, half and full. The degrees of shade are definitely open to interpretation. Just as native people have many words to describe snow, the English language provides many descriptive words to describe shade.

PARTIAL SHADE

This refers to shade that does not last all day—generally, areas that receive full sun for three to six hours a day. This is the easiest form of shade to work with and, in very warm areas of the country, many sun-loving plants actually prefer a few hours of shade in the mid- to late afternoon as their foliage can virtually fry in full sun. Trees, vines, fences and other garden structures may also produce the equivalent of partial shade, as long as the sun filters through to a degree.

Giant 'Abiqua Drinking Gourd' hosta adds texture and drama to the shade garden.

Green is the dominant colour in a shade garden, so look for plants with a variety of *foliage* colours, sizes, shapes, heights and textures to add interest. For instance, contrast chartreuse coral bells (*Heuchera*) such as 'Lime Rickey' with a rich red-and-lime coleus such as 'Bronze Pagoda'. Glossy-leaved plants, with their reflective quality, have more impact than matte or fuzzy leaves in the shade. *Avoid plants with fleshy, grey-green leaves-they tend to like full sun and dryness.*

DAPPLED SHADE

Sometimes referred to as open, filtered or light shade, dappled shade is created by light filtering through the canopy of deciduous trees or open structures such as wooden lattice or lath.

Trees with small open leaves such as honey locust and birch allow quite a lot of light through, as will trees with very high canopies. Buildings or tall evergreens that are some distance away may also create light shade,

A cutleaf Japanese maple and 'Annabelle' hydrangea thrive in dappled shade.

similar to dappled shade.

Because the angle of the sun changes throughout the day, areas with dappled shade may receive an hour or two of full sun, but even when they are in shade, there is still enough ambient light to support many types of plants. The degree of shade also changes with the season. Deciduous trees allow lots of sunlight through their bare branches in late fall, winter and early spring, offering increasing shade as they leaf out.

FULL SHADE

This type of shade describes an area that receives no direct sunlight, only diffused light. You might find this type of shade on the north side of a wall or under densely leaved deciduous trees such as mature maples and oaks. Plant choices for full shade are limited to those that are truly shade-tolerant. Trees with very large leaves such as the Norway maple may cast too much shade (even though it may be only during summer) for anything other than cast-iron plants like lily of the valley to grow under them. Also, trees with shallow roots—again, the Norway maple is a prime example—will consume much of the water and nutrients of the surrounding soil, creating difficult, dry planting conditions.

Dense Shade   Full Shade

Partial Shade   Dappled Shade

DENSE SHADE

Sometimes called deep or heavy shade, this is the most challenging shade for a gardener. It describes an area that receives very little or no light year-round. It is found under mature evergreen trees, beside buildings or on the floor of a mature woodland. Tall buildings can create a great expanse of dense shade, particularly on their north sides. Dense shade under trees is usually very dry due to limited exposure to rainfall and the abundance of mature tree roots. Very little can be grown in these conditions.

A shady corner of my previous backyard with, from left to right, Japanese spurge, hosta and Lamium.

KEY ELEMENT

SPRING BULBS FOR SHADE

Bulbs in the shade garden are best planted in the dappled shade of deciduous trees. The sun coming through the branches in early spring is perfect for encouraging snowdrops, crocuses, daffodils, fritillaries, glory of the snow, grape hyacinths and the like to flower before the tree canopy is in full leaf. I find some of the best spring-flowering bulbs for this purpose are those labeled "good for naturalizing" on the package. Look for them at your retailer in the autumn.

White impatiens, draws attention to dark corners.

Light-coloured flowers, especially white, shine more brilliantly in a shady garden than dark colours like red, purple or deep blue. Silvery foliage plants such as *Lamium, Brunnera* and *Pulmonaria* will also brighten a shady spot.

Plant fewer varieties of flowers in greater numbers to create large swaths of colour as subtle tone variations and individual flowers tend to get lost in the shade. Use plants that will naturalize in the setting (generally plants that are vigorous growers and sometimes aggressive). Seek out shade-loving native plants that self-seed—they will naturally find their optimum growing conditions in your garden.

Coral bells (Heuchera) prefer partial shade.

Hardy to Zone 5, Japanese spurge (Pachysandra) is a terrific full-shade groundcover.

STRATEGIES FOR THE SHADE GARDEN

Don't be afraid to take up the shade-garden challenge; the rewards can be huge. Here are some ideas to help you make the most of your shady area or areas:

PICK THE RIGHT PLANTS

There are both annuals and perennials that are shade-lovers. You will get the greatest variety of bloom time, colour and shape if you incorporate both into your garden design. Perennials and bulbs are particularly useful for early spring colour. If you plant bulbs with shade-lovers like hostas, ferns, astilbe and lobelia, the latter will take over in summer and hide the bulbs' dying foliage. Many perennials that do well in the shade are low-growing types that have wonderful leaf colours and shapes but less spectacular flowers. They can make excellent groundcovers or border plants.

MITIGATE YOUR SHADE

Create some sunny spots or change full shade into dappled shade if possible by hiring an arborist or professional tree trimmer to thin out large trees or limb them up so that more light gets through the branches.

You can increase your planting options by reflecting more light into your garden. Consider painting walls, fences and hard furnishings white or pale colours. If you are using paving stones, bricks, gravel or chipped stones for paths, select those lightest in colour. In colder growing zones, take advantage of stone or brick walls that retain heat and plan your beds for areas of the garden that have the lightest shade.

In really dense shade, your best bet is not to try the impossible. Instead, devote this space to hard furnishings such as benches, outdoor sculpture, bird feeders and a bird bath) and cover the ground with attractive mulches, paving stones or pebbles. If you want to have some colour here, use mobile containers with plants that can be moved from the dense shade to a sunny spot when needed.

A mirrored gazing globe adds sparkle.

TEND THE SOIL

If the shade is created by trees, their hungry, thirsty roots are depleting the soil of nutrients and drying it out. Add organic matter annually to build up a layer of rich humusy soil on top of the tree roots. Remember that the vast majority of a tree's roots are in the top four feet of soil, which means that your plants will be struggling to put down their own tender roots through a mass of fibrous tree roots.

In shady spots with heavy soil where there are no trees, the ground can be boggy. Add sharp sand to improve drainage: about 10 kilos (22 pounds) per square metre (10 square feet) dug down 25 centimetres (10 inches) will quickly make a huge improvement.

Shade reduces evaporation caused by sun and heat, and the resulting dampness can lead to disease such as mould, mildew and rot. To avoid this, place plants a little farther apart in the shade to aid air circulation and always remove dead foliage as soon as you see it.

Also keep an eye on organic mulches. If you suspect mould or fungus is growing in the mulch, turn the mulch over with a garden rake to allow the damp parts to dry out, or remove the mulch altogether for a time (this may be a good idea during periods of continued precipitation).

In dry shade, look for plants that are both shade- and drought-tolerant. You may also want to employ some sort of in-ground watering system, or use soaker and weeping hoses covered with mulch to provide consistent, adequate moisture. But if you opt for the in-ground watering system, keep the switch on "manual" and water only as required.

PERENNIAL GROUNDCOVERS FOR THE SHADE GARDEN

VARIETY	HARDINESS ZONE
Allegheny spurge (*Pachysandra procumbens*)	5
Barren strawberry (*Waldsteinia ternata*)	5
Canada wild ginger (*Asarum canadense*)	4
Carpet bugleweed (*Ajuga* x *tenorii*)	2
Creeping dead nettle (*Lamium maculatum*)	3
Creeping Jenny (*Lysimachia nummularia*)	2
Japanese spurge (*Pachysandra terminalis*)	5
Lily of the valley (*Convallaria majalis*)	2
Sweet woodruff (*Galium odoratum*)	3

Shade-loving perennials thrive where grass has little success.

Black walnut trees provide lovely dappled shade but their roots secrete a substance called juglone that is toxic to many plants. So be sure to look for juglone-tolerant plants such as ferns, phlox, sweet woodruff, trilliums, daffodils, hostas, viburnums and hemlocks. Before planting, add lots of organic matter to the soil and make certain the drainage is excellent.

LOOK AT LAWN OPTIONS

Many books and articles recommend forgoing a lawn if you have a shade garden. I am an unapologetic fan of lawns—I like the look of the even green carpet and find it a wonderful transition between flower beds, trees and other garden elements. As for the environmental concerns that some gardeners express about lawns, well, there are environmentally friendly alternatives to the traditional treatment of lawns. If you are a lawn fan too, by all means try establishing a shade lawn. But take into account the challenges it presents. (See Chapter 12 for more on shade lawns.)

If you have full or dense shade, or have had no success with a shade lawn, consider alternatives. Mulches, such as natural pine or cedar bark or crushed stone, make attractive groundcoverings in dense shade. Shade-loving groundcovers like spurge, periwinkle, dead nettle (*Lamium*) and *Euonymus* are good choices for full, partial or dappled shade. In very cold regions, consider using climbing vines as groundcovers, for example, Virginia creeper and species clematis.

Whatever your shady situation, keep in mind that adding some green, growing plants to a shady part of your yard will add humidity and oxygen on a hot summer day. Not a bad place to be when the rest of the neighbourhood is baking.

KEY ELEMENT

CONTAINER SOLUTION
Container gardening is the answer to the problem of planting under trees where digging is difficult. Use new, quality potting soil at the time of planting and set the pot on blocks or pot feet to allow good air circulation and to prevent tree roots from migrating into the soil of the pot.

Solid green ground cover cools down a garden and makes this sitting area particularly relaxing and inviting.

City gardeners can find inspiration in public gardens such as Toronto's Music Garden.

CHAPTER THREE
The City Garden

I love city gardens for their intensity.

Come late spring, I always attend some of the marvellous public tours of private gardens that take place in the downtown area. These tours always include some of the best gardens in an urban neighbourhood. I am fascinated by the creativity that designers and homeowners display when it comes to gardening in small spaces. The challenges bring out the best of our resourcefulness and creativity.

City dwellers have the unique opportunity to create a very personal environment in their outdoor space. Though urban spaces are generally small, it is possible to transform them into beautiful and intimate gardens for relaxing, entertaining or enjoying family activities. But this cannot be achieved without careful planning and some special considerations. A skillful design that fits the space can make a small garden appear much larger.

UPSIDE, DOWNSIDE

In a small landscape, everything is up close and personal, from flowers and foliage to hard furnishings and structures. The focus is on detail, so plant selection is of utmost importance; any plant that doesn't fit, in size or colour, will stand out. Space is at a premium: every plant should bear

The repetition of canna lilies, geum and yellow coneflowers provides rhythm and unity in the garden.

close inspection and have something to offer in as many seasons as possible. On the downside, areas of neglect

One well-chosen evergreen provides a focal point.

are equally noticeable: overgrown shrubs, leggy annuals, spent flowers and thriving weeds are sure to catch the eye. While small gardens demand careful attention, they also are easier to maintain than their suburban and rural counterparts.

KEY ELEMENT

GO FOR FOLIAGE

To make your city garden really work for you, choose annuals and perennials that have unusual and interesting leaves as well as flowers. While there are many excellent flowering plants to choose from, truth is that there is no such thing as a perennial that blooms nonstop all season long. Gorgeous foliage will provide a constant feast for the eyes, even from the vantage point of your favourite garden lounger. In a small space, opt for subtle colours, as very bright hues can be overpowering.

Low hedges divide the space and make it seem larger.

CREATE LEVELS AND ROOMS

As many interior designers will tell you, sometimes by dividing a space you can actually make it seem bigger. Don't be afraid to create a few distinct areas or little "rooms" within your small garden. Low hedges of boxwood or dwarf spirea are terrific to make "walls" defining the rooms and adding structure to the space. A change in grade- a step or two onto a different level- is also an effective way of dividing space to make it seem larger.

URBAN GARDEN STRATEGIES

CREATE PRIVACY

A common goal in an urban environment is to create privacy, often through screens or fences.

A privacy screen, dwarf conifers and a quietly flowing fountain create personal space in the centre of the city.

When choosing these permanent structures, think carefully about what will be most attractive as well as practical, as they will likely be visible from every vantage point. It is worth stretching the budget to get the effect that you want.

Solid screens and fences may offer the most privacy, but it is important that they are open enough to allow sunlight and air to penetrate. A garden with good air circulation is less susceptible to disease and moss and cools down more effectively in the heat of summer.

SOFTEN BOUNDARIES

Often city gardens are surrounded by tall walls or neighbouring buildings that loom over the space. Mitigate this by planting a specimen tree or tall shrub; the greenery will act as a soft backdrop to your garden and make the forbidding walls seem to recede.

GROW VERTICAL

Vertical gardening adds another dimension to a small yard and creates the illusion of more space by adding height and drawing the eye upward. Vines and climbing plants can be trained to grow up trellises

An exuberant clematis draws the eye upward. (Royal Botanical Gardens, Burlington, Ontario).

and arbours, as well as sheds, garages, walls and fences. There are many plant possibilities, for sun or shade, featuring colour, texture and often fragrance to beat the band!

An inviting stepped entryway at Cedar Ridge Creative Centre.

USE EVERY BIT OF SPACE

Be creative with your use of space. Are there any areas of hidden space on your site? A small pocket of soil at the base of the garage wall might be the spot for a vine-covered trellis. That ribbon of turf alongside the driveway might become home to a narrow flower bed. Is there enough light and good soil in the space between your house and your neighbour's to plant a luscious shade garden?

If you have lawn at the front of the house, why not transform it into a front-yard garden? Not only will you create an attractive and inviting introduction to your property, but you'll also have additional planting space!

You can fill it with flowers but don't be afraid to plant vegetables there, too. You'll have a feast for the eyes, as well as the table.

A shady side yard is lush with grass and subtle blooms.

Here are two very different substitutes for a traditional lawn. One (above) is a flower-filled "cottage-style garden", and the other (left) is a brand-new "xeriscape", an approach that emphasizes less water use.

BLOCK OUT CITY NOISE

In many small garden designs, I recommend the addition of a water feature such as a fountain or water-circulating birdbath. The sound of trickling water helps to muffle noise from the street and, even better, attracts birds to your garden while providing a relaxing aural backdrop. To avoid worries of mosquitoes and West Nile virus, try installing a bubbler (a rock with a hole drilled through it). The water comes up from a hidden pump, trickles over the stone and into the pebble-covered reservoir, so you get the sound but no open water.

the plants') needs. Retailers have answered the demand for colourful, durable and attractive containers so gardeners have plenty to choose from. For my recipe for successful containers, see Chapter 14.

Large tropicals add drama to a patio.

CONSIDER CONTAINERS

Containers are useful in every city garden, but particularly so where the space is limited to a patio or deck. In containers, you can change the plants from year to year, as well as from season to season to extend the colour and interest. Containers give you complete control over soil and watering conditions, and they're portable so you can change their location according to your (and

Shade - loving begonias and impatiens fill a sumptuous basket.

KEEP ELEMENTS IN SCALE

Choose hardscaping, plants, furnishings and accessories to suit the size of your space. Do you like the idea of a shady gazebo but don't have the room? Build a small arbour or pergola with a bench underneath instead. You'll get the same effect, just on a smaller scale.

Similarly, choose plants carefully, checking the information on the tags to make sure their ultimate size will fit the garden.

All successful gardens have something happening in every season, which means you need a variety of plants—a challenge in a small garden where you can't have the wide groupings of the same plant that you might in a large space. Diversity in plant material will not only give your landscape increased interest but also result in a healthier garden with fewer pests and diseases.

To squeeze more plants into your space, choose small or dwarf forms— smaller spring-flowering bulbs such as crocuses and species tulips rather than large Darwin hybrid tulips, for example. There are dwarf varieties of all sorts of perennials, as well as woody plants.

Trees and shrubs are essential even in a small garden, but should be chosen and placed judiciously. Be prepared to amend the soil with generous quantities of compost or composted cattle manure (steer manure, if you live in the Canadian west) on a regular basis.

This tasteful arbour and bench perfectly suit the scale of the space.

MY FAVOURITE SELECTIONS FOR SMALL SPACES

TREES	SHRUBS	PERENNIALS
Standard purpleleaf sandcherry (*Prunus cistena*) Zone 3	Dwarf fragrant viburnum (*Viburnum ferreri* 'Nanum') Zone 5	Fern-leaf bleeding heart (*Dicentra formosa*) Zone 3
Weeping peashrub (*Caragana arborescens* 'Pendula') Zone 3	Dwarf lilac (*Syringa meyeri*) Zone 3	Dwarf bellflower (*Campanula cochlearifolia*) Zone 3
PeeGee hydrangea (*Hydrangea paniculata* 'Grandiflora') Zone 4	Miniature mockorange (*Philadelphus virginalis* 'Miniature Snowflake') Zone 5	Coral bells (*Heuchera*) Zone 5
Standard dwarf lilac (*Syringa meyeri*) Zone 3	Dwarf burning bush (*Euonymus alatus* 'Compactus') Zone 3	Primrose (*Primula*) Zone 4
Flowering almond (*Prunus triloba*) Zone 2		Dwarf hosta (*Hosta*) Zone 3
		Silver mound artemisia (*Artemisia schmidtiana* 'Nana') Zone 3

The Ford Truck Plant's green roof.

HIGH-RISE GREENING
The rooftop garden has taken on a whole new meaning in recent years. No longer just a place to sit, surrounded by lovely plants, the term "green roof" relates to a functioning structure on the top of buildings that is covered with plants. Often a monoculture of tough plants such as sedum is used (as is the case at the Ford Truck Plant in Dearborn, Michigan, the largest green roof in the world).

The headquarters for the World Green Building Council, focusing on sustainable living, is right here in Canada at the Living City Campus at the Kortright Centre for Conservation in Woodbridge, just northwest of Toronto. **For more information, go to www.worldgbc.org.**

BALCONY & ROOFTOP GARDENS

401 Richmond Street in Toronto is a model roof top garden!

In recent years, many new condos and townhouses feature both balcony and rooftop areas that are landscaped as soon as the units are occupied. In fact, more and more townhouses are being designed specifically so that residents each have their own rooftop garden. There are a number of organizations that are promoting rooftop and balcony gardening as an important part of urban environmental renewal. They point out that these kinds of gardens not only maximize the use of urban space but also provide a restorative green haven for city dwellers, additional oxygen to the air and even a potential source of fresh produce for the urban population.

If you are gardening on a balcony or rooftop, you are almost certainly gardening in a microclimate-that is, different growing conditions from the landscape at ground level around you. As with any garden design, it is necessary to assess those conditions before you begin your garden installation.

SUN/SHADE
Consider which way your balcony faces and when it receives direct sunlight. Morning shade with afternoon sun (west exposure) presents challenges for gardeners as plants stay cool throughout the morning only to be exposed to the hottest sun in the afternoon. If, however, your space gets morning sun and afternoon shade (eastern exposure), you have the perfect spot for plants that like partial shade.

If your outdoor space is overshadowed by other buildings or by balconies above you, there could be enough reflected or ambient light to support a shade garden. If you have a rooftop in full sun, consider installing retractable awnings against walls or high railings to shade your plantings during the hottest parts of the day. Structures such as pergolas, mini-gazebos or lathe enclosures provide cooling shade and a cozy feeling of intimacy.

Colourful annuals relish a sunny exposure.

Remember that since balconies and rooftops are almost invariably bordered by brick or concrete walls and floors, they retain heat. When temperatures at ground level are perfectly comfortable, the growing conditions a few storeys up may be much hotter as the sun heats up the exposed walls and floors. One advantage is that while your ground-floor neighbours in a city like Ottawa or Montreal are gardening in Zone 4 conditions, your Zone 5 plants are thriving in their warmer home.

While this increased exposure to the sun on a balcony/rooftop provides an environment equal to one zone warmer during the growing season, winter is another matter. Greater exposure to wind and subzero temperatures can make your balcony/rooftop a zone colder!

Containerized plants can be rearranged or replanted individually, as you wish.

Arranging containers in close groups will also help prevent moisture loss.

Avoid hanging baskets that are 25 centimetres (10 inches) or less in diameter. If you live higher than the second storey they will dry out very quickly and might even become airborne in a strong wind. I now use only hanging baskets that are a minimum of 35-centimetres (14 inches) in diameter rather than the traditional 25-centimetres (10-inch) plastic baskets.

Coir brick- just add water!

WIND AND WATER

Another important factor in balcony or rooftop gardening is wind. The higher you live, the greater the effects of the wind. Your garden will dry out very quickly, so use bigger containers that can hold more lightweight soil, and water frequently. You may find you have to water your containers every day in the heat of summer. To help reduce watering, add coir (coconut fiber) to your planting mix, and apply a pine or cedar bark mulch at least five centimetres (two inches) deep to minimize evaporation from the soil.

The green roof at the Toronto Botanical Garden— on a very hot day! (www.torontobotanicalgarden.ca)

On rooftops, consider creating additional barriers using hardy shrubs, evergreens, fencing or other structures to serve as windbreaks. Even so, conditions can be tough, so choose hardy plant material.

When grown on balconies and rooftops, evergreen trees and shrubs must be sheltered and protected from wind damage. Even if you are not using evergreens, you might want to create some wind protection for your garden. Plexiglas® sheets can be attached to open railings of balconies, or canvas runners can be threaded through the railing uprights.

Hardy vines can be grown along the railings. Just make sure that the containers they are planted in are big enough—at least a half barrel in size— to accommodate the roots of a mature vine and that the containers can take the rigours of the freeze/thaw cycle each winter.

CONTAINERS

If you are planning a garden on a rooftop or balcony, you will most certainly be gardening in some kind of container. Keep in mind, however, that unlike the backyard gardener who can use cast-iron planters with abandon, be cautious about the weight of the containers you use. Not only do you not want to heave a 22-kilo (50-pound) planter up a flight of stairs to the roof, but you also don't want that planter, further weighed down by soil and water, to come crashing through your roof!

Before planning your garden, check with your landlord or builder about weight restrictions for your balcony or rooftop. Use lightweight soil mixes or soilless mixes (vermiculite and peat-moss-based mixes work well). Choose lightweight containers —remember, if the soil is kept moist and gravel or stone chips are used to add drainage at the bottom of the container, even polyresin containers can be heavy enough to be stable and wind-resistant. Alternatively, if your container is made of a heavier material, use lightweight drainage material such as Styrofoam packing pieces at the bottom rather than stones or gravel.

Many rooftop gardeners use very large containers that are essentially raised beds or boxes constructed of lumber and often handsomely finished. These work very well on rooftops as they can be planted more densely than smaller containers and do not dry out as quickly. For perennials, the additional soil also provides insulation over the winter.

Sheets of Styrofoam used to line the walls of a large container are very useful. The additional insulation helps to slow the potentially damaging effects of the wind, frost and dry spells. I recommend Styrofoam sheets 2.5 to five centimetres (one to two inches) thick. Large planting boxes can give a variety of looks to a rooftop, from traditional to contemporary. If your rooftop garden plans are very ambitious, I recommend that you talk to a contractor about additional waterproofing and insulation for your roof.

Also, be cautious if you're placing window boxes that hang outside the railing over the street. You'll have to make sure that water and/or the plants themselves don't end up on the ground (or passersby) below. You'll get a better view of window boxes set *inside* the railing, and watering and weeding will be easier too.

While all urban gardeners have to learn to work within the limitations of space, there is a great opportunity to exercise your creative muscles and have fun!

This clever gardener in LaRonge, Sask., has created privacy on her balcony, but can always move the planter if she wishes.

Well-amended soil results in flourishing flowers and shrubs.

CHAPTER FOUR
The Suburban Garden

A friend of mine likes to say, "When you live in the suburbs, you need a rich fantasy life." I like to say that a rich fantasy life is part of what a great gardening experience is all about!

When they were originally conceived, I believe that the suburbs were intended to combine the best qualities of urban living and a life in the country, without the long drive into the city. Truth is, suburban gardeners enjoy less noise on average than city dwellers without the endless space that you can have on the family farm and the resulting maintenance issues associated with it. I think that life in the suburbs can be a wonderful experience for gardeners.

When I speak of suburban gardens, I am referring to those of single-family homes in relatively new developments. These yards are generally devoid of much landscaping so the best place to start is with a plan. In many ways, it's easier to start with a clean slate than work around existing plants or resolve inherited problems. You have a far wider range of design options, better access for machinery and materials, and the fun of creating a garden from scratch that you can truly call your own.

The most important thing about a plan for a new garden is that you know what you want to accomplish with the yard so you can divide the space to make it both beautiful and functional.

Create a list of priorities, such as a children's play area, seating, specialty gardens such as herb, vegetable or cutting gardens, lawn

Mix containers with permanent gardens.

A red and white theme = a proud Canadian!

for recreation, or a barbecue/entertainment area, etc. You may not be able to include everything, but a wish list is a vital first step in garden planning, especially if you bring in a designer or landscape architect to draw up a plan. He or she will be able to tell you what is feasible and help you translate your ideas into reality (see Chapter 1 for more on the design process).

SUBURBAN SOIL

KEY ELEMENT

ADVICE FOR NEW HOMEOWNERS
If you are buying a new home, I suggest that you put into your offer to purchase a condition stating that you will supply the topsoil. This should shave $500 to $1,000 off your purchase price. However, you will invest more than that amount of money in new triple mix that you can acquire from a reliable local supplier. The key here is "reliable" -be sure to purchase the highest-quality soil you can get. This is the best investment you can make in your future Eden—and gardening will be a pleasure.

Gardens are built from the ground up, literally. Before any garden plan can be implemented, you need to have a solid foundation of good soil —a particular challenge for suburban gardeners. When new housing developments are put in, the first visible step is the scraping away of the topsoil from the building site. Home-builders remove the valuable topsoil before digging foundations and driving large equipment over the site throughout the construction process. When the homes are complete, the developers spread a layer of topsoil over the fresh grade. This leaves new home-buyers with a severely compacted yard and a thin layer of "developer's topsoil."

To create a garden on such a site, you will need to amend the soil significantly. Break up the compacted base by digging deep, and loosen the soil with a garden fork or a rototiller. Add a layer of organic compost spread five centimetres (two inches) thick and till it in to improve moisture retention, aeration and drainage. (See Chapter 13 for more on determining the kind of soil you have and how to improve it.)

The ancient maidenhair tree (Ginkgo biloba) was "discovered" in the courtyard of a Buddhist temple. It makes a fine specimen tree in any garden.

When space is limited, you want to choose trees for the landscape carefully. The best advice I can give you when planting a new tree is: think in terms of a five- to 10-year horizon and plant for the future. There is no point in planting a tree that will outgrow the yard within five years because you will be back to square one when it is removed. Choose a tree based on its mature size and site requirements.

PLANTING TREES

You can often judge the age of a housing development by estimating the maturity of its trees. Most new subdivisions are missing the beauty and history of mature trees, so a tree is usually one of the first things that new homeowners want to plant. Trees not only provide shade for us and habitat for birds but also improve the air quality, reduce rainwater runoff and increase property values.

When planting near a driveway or pool, it is best to choose a "clean" tree, one that does not drop fruit or sap; otherwise, your car's finish is at risk. Plant a large tree at least seven metres (21 feet) away from your house and foundations, and watch out for utility lines and overhead wires. Water your tree diligently for at least the first year; the primary cause of a tree's premature death is shortage of water in its early life. (See Chapter 14 for how to plant trees successfully.)

SCREENING FOR PRIVACY

Creating some privacy becomes a priority the first time you try to enjoy your yard at the same time your neighbours are outdoors. Fences are one solution and can offer screening, a pleasing structural frame for the garden and a handsome backdrop for plantings. Also consider strategically placed trellises planted with perennial vines, which will add colour, texture and often fragrance to your garden.

SUGGESTED TREES FOR SUBURBAN GARDENS

VARIETY	HARDINESS ZONE	DESCRIPTION
Maidenhair tree (*Ginkgo biloba*)	4	Pollution-tolerant; disease-resistant; slow-growing.
Littleleaf linden (*Tilia cordata*)	3	Tolerant of heat and compacted soil.
Ash (*Fraxinus*)	3	Transplants easily; very adaptable; tolerates a wide range of soil conditions. Choose seedless varieties to avoid litter problems.
Pin oak (*Quercus palustris*)	4	Transplants easily; tolerates wet clay soils but prefers moist, rich, well-drained soil.
Japanese pagoda tree (*Sophora japonica*)	5	Medium-sized tree with elegant foliage; blooms in summer; tolerates urban conditions and drought.
Thornless honey locust (*Gleditsia triacanthos* var. *inermis*)	4	Easy to transplant; withstands a wide range of conditions and is salt-tolerant.

Handsome and effective privacy screens. (Image courtesy of Pathways to Perennials. www.pathwaystoperennials.com)

Wooden lattice and panels are handsome and effective privacy screens. (Image courtesy of Pathways to Perennials. www. pathwaystoperennials.com)

A cedar hedge makes a reliable screen in almost all growing zones.

Of course, the perfect green screen is a hedge. It's important to make the proper plant choices for a hedge as it is a principal feature of the garden and can be a big investment. Also, some hedges such as privet that needs regular trimming are higher maintenance than others. Consider whether you want the year-round screen that evergreens give you, or a deciduous hedge that might offer flowers, berries or fall colour as a bonus.

*"A hedge between…
keeps friendship green"*

SUGGESTED PLANTS FOR PRIVACY

VARIETY	HARDINESS ZONE	DESCRIPTION
Eastern white cedar (*Thuja occidentalis*) [usually for hedging]	3	Very adaptable evergreen; gives year-round privacy; full sun to light shade.
Yew (*Taxus*) [hedging]	4	Lustrous evergreen; takes pruning and shearing; partial shade.
Alpine currant (*Ribes alpinum*) [hedging]	3	Can be sheared for formal appearance; sun or shade.
Amur privet (*Ligustrum amurense*) [hedging]	3	Grown for its dense foliage; tolerates heavy pruning.
Amur maple (*Acer ginnala*) [shrub barrier or informal hedge]	3	Small tree with dense foliage; very tough; vivid scarlet autumn colour.
Clematis (*Clematis* spp.) [flowering twining vine]	Varies with variety	Varies with variety Grow on chain link fence, arbour or trellis; full sun with roots shaded.
Climbing hydrangea (*Hydrangea anomala* ssp. *petiolaris*) [flowering self-clinging vine]	4	Train along a fence; can grow 25 metres (80 feet);shade or sun.
Boston ivy (*Parthenocissus tricuspidata*) [self-clinging vine]	4	Train along a fence; can grow up to 10 metres (30 feet); vigorous grower; red fall colour.

An expanse of verdant lawn is ideal for a family game of croquet.

If your top priority is a children's play area, you will likely want to limit the amount of space set aside for gardens in favour of lawn. Watch the neighbourhood children the next time they gather for a game of catch or tag. Nine times out of 10 they will flock to the yard with the most open lawn space! If children and pets are going to be using the lawn, it is even more crucial to follow an organic lawn-care program; you don't want to expose them to any sort of chemicals or pesticides. It is entirely possible to have an attractive, problem-free lawn that is kind to not only to your family but also the environment. (See Chapter 12 for more on lawns and easy lawn care.)

To make your ornamental gardens kid-friendly, focus on hardy shrubs planted around the perimeter of the yard. Children enjoy open space to run without worrying about stepping on mom's favourite plant. More elaborate gardens can perhaps be installed in side yards, or in the front yard to enhance curb appeal.

Also consider giving the children a little garden of their own where they can plant quick-growing, appealing plants such as sunflowers, nasturtiums, mini pumpkins and cherry tomatoes. Or make a teepee out of half a dozen long poles and plant scarlet runner beans and morning glories at their base; the vines will grow up to cover the teepee, creating a secret, kids-only place inside.

KEY ELEMENT

RECIPE FOR DISCOURAGING CATS
If neighbourhood cats are using your garden as a litter box, here's a scat-cat recipe: Mix 1 large onion, 1 whole garlic bulb, 1 tablespoon Tabasco sauce and 1 litre of water in a blender. Pour on the areas of the garden frequented by cats. Repeat this process after a heavy rainfall or every 10 days until the cats have found a washroom elsewhere.

Oliver enjoys a shady spot in the garden.

Dogs really appreciate a nice stretch of lawn, but their urine (with its high nitrogen content) can burn the grass. To prevent these brown patches, hose down (ideally within an hour) the area where the dog has gone. Putting more water in the dog's kibble is supposed to help, too. Alternatively, create a separate little gravel-covered area and train the dog to go there. This is easily washed down and will spare your lawn.

PET- FRIENDLY GARDENS

Gardens and pets can happily co-exist with some careful planning. Consider the following when creating outdoor space for your pets:

- Provide shade for relief from the sun, and always have a supply of fresh water.

- Install a solid fence at least 1.2 metres (four feet) high. Bury 15 centimetres (six inches) of the fence below grade to deter digging and tunneling under the fence.

- Invest in large plants, which are more likely to withstand canine traffic in the yard.

- Plant groundcovers or spread mulch to avoid leaving exposed soil. Both dogs and cats view bare soil as an invitation to dig.

- Use sod rather than sowing grass seed. Sod will establish more quickly and be more resilient.

- Dogs need exercise and a long path through the yard is a good option. A surface of finely shredded cedar bark mulch is comfortable on paws and travels less than pea gravel or bark chips.

- Avoid plants with thorns, which can cause injury, and be very cautious about poisonous plants such as castor bean or hellebore.

For a detailed list of toxic plants, visit… www.aspca.org/toxicplants.

LOWER MAINTENANCE

Living in the suburbs often means a long commute to and from work each day, leaving little time for yard work or savouring the joys of gardening. But there are ways to reduce maintenance and still enjoy a family garden. First and foremost is mulching, which reduces weeds, watering and fertilizing, and keeps the plants happy to boot. (See Chapter 16 for more on mulch.)

Choose plants that suit the conditions of your site, that are tough, drought-tolerant and pest-resistant, and that don't need a lot of maintaining (dividing, pruning, deadheading, etc.). It pays to do a bit of research before heading out to the garden centre, but don't hesitate to ask the folks there for suggestions. (See Chapter 5 for more time-saving tips.

Tough, drought-tolerant plants such as Rudbeckia and coneflowers are ideal for a low-maintenance garden.

'Karl Foerster' feather reed grass.

Bleeding heart.

Japanese painted fern.

'Amber Waves' coral bells.

Black-eyed Susans.

'Patriot' hosta.

MY FAVOURITE LOW-MAINTENANCE PERENNIALS

FOR PART SHADE

Astilbe (*Astilbe* x *rosea*)	Zone 5
Bleeding heart (*Dicentra* 'Luxuriant')	Zone 4
Coral bells (*Heuchera*)	Zone 5
Hosta (*Hosta*)	Zone 3
Japanese painted fern (*Athyrium niponicum*)	Zone 4

FOR SUN

Black-eyed Susan (*Rudbeckia hirta*)	Zone 5
Coreopsis (*Coreopsis grandiflora*)	Zone 4
Daylily (*Hemerocallis* 'Stella d'Oro')	Zone 3
Feather reed grass (*Calamagrostis* x *acutiflora* 'Karl Foerster')	Zone 4
Purple coneflower (*Echinacea purpurea*)	Zone 3

Purple coneflower.

Red and yellow daylilies.

Our flower- filled front yard.

CHAPTER FIVE
The Country Garden

After gardening in the suburbs for 25 years, I am now a "country" gardener. Mary and I moved to her family farm, built a house there and now I enjoy a lovely 10-acre garden. From my brief experience, I can tell you that gardening in the wide open spaces is very different from the confined space of a suburban lot, but I see it as a wonderful opportunity.

COUNTRY GARDEN STRATEGIES

There aren't a lot of books around on the sole subject of the "big country garden" so here are a few ideas to keep in mind if you have the gift of space.

PLANT IN WIDE SWATHS

With a large lot, you have the luxury of creating dramatic sweeps of colour by planting large numbers of the same flower. (Just one or two flowers will look lost on the big canvas.) You can also use statuesque plants—big specimen perennials such as Joe-Pye weed, white fleece flower and giant maiden grass—that would overpower a small garden.

If you do want a more subtle look than large groupings of plants provide, consider a meadow-type garden with a select number of flowers mixed together over a wide area. A true meadow (not the kind that comes in a can) takes some effort to establish but is a glorious sight with its tapestry of grasses and flowers. (See Chapter 6 for more on meadow gardens.)

USE REPETITION

Repeating elements within a garden to create a pattern or a rhythm is a sound design technique no matter what size your garden is, but it is especially helpful if you are trying to unify a large space. Repeat large

Swaths of black-eyed Susans and 'Victoria Blue' salvia—in the country, plant in quantity!

elements such as clusters of shrubs or groups of trees, and small elements such as mounding border plantings of bellflowers or alyssum, as your space allows. I've seen gardens where a particular shape was repeated to great effect—for example, spheres of allium, globe cedars and boxwood. Or you can repeat one or two colours, whether in plants or structures (see the next item).

My "hill" of purple coneflowers.

A fence and mixed border create a more intimate space within the whole garden.

CHOOSE DOMINANT COLOURS

To capture and hold attention, consider using a particular colour or colour combination that will echo throughout the garden. Blues and yellows, for example, or blazing shades of red and orange will make bold statements that will draw the eye through the space. Grey-green foliage or white blossoms can act as foils, linking the stronger colours and also providing some gentle respite.

CREATE GENEROUS BORDERS

If planned and planted thoughtfully, garden borders can give your large property a more "homey" feeling. By planting generous borders on all sides of the yard, what I call framing, you'll create a feeling of intimacy that many large yards lack.

In smaller gardens, the depth and length of borders may be dictated by the size of your lot. But in a larger garden, you can frame your whole yard with the garden border. Begin your design process by looking at the views from the windows in your most frequently used rooms. These views should be framed and enhanced by plants and structures. Draw a rough plan of your property and the house placement. Using a grid made up of straight lines, determine where those frames should fall and where you want major pathways. Avoid blocking desirable views. Establishing a basic geometry so that major elements are aligned will give the garden a strong underlying structure. Within this grid of straight lines, you can create curved beds and walkways that are secondary to the main path system.

Keep the borders proportional to the size of the overall garden. Place shade or flowering trees in the remaining lawn area, being careful to provide them with room to grow without blocking attractive views from your home.

DIVIDE THE SPACE

To add variety and give the feeling of a more intimate space, divide your country garden into a series of smaller gardens or "rooms," using the grid you have laid out (See "Create generous borders," this page). These rooms can be defined by hedges, fencing, trellises, pathways, or hard furnishings.

Berms, groundcovers and flower borders can also mark the transition from one area of the garden to another. Arbours planted with vines can act as doorways. A series of attractive arbours will draw visitors on a tour of your garden without your ever having to leave your lounge chair.

KEY ELEMENT

MAKE BORDER CROSSINGS

The deeper the garden border, the more likely you will want to add paths, stepping stones or other means of allowing you to move into the borders to weed, cultivate or carry out other maintenance. These practical maintenance paths will be hidden as plants mature and grow over them.

The dahlia garden at Butchart Gardens in Victoria, BC, is not your average border, but it is inspiring.

Trees, shrubs and evergreens create a low-maintenance tapestry at the Royal Botanical Gardens in Burlington, Ontario.

MAINTAINING THE COUNTRY GARDEN

There are several approaches or tricks that you can use to work with nature to produce a splendid-looking garden without having to quit your day job to look after it.

PICK PLANTS THAT NATURALIZE

Consider the soil and the growing conditions on your land—from the long, hot summers on the Prairies to the cool, late springs of the East Coast—and choose plants whose needs match those

An arbour defines the space and invites you to move through the garden.

conditions. The plants will thrive, either self-seeding or producing many off-shoots. Plants that spread on their own (i.e., naturalize) will save you a lot of work.

I think of the wonderful display of lupines that I see in the Maritimes every summer and I am reminded of the many gardeners I've met from there who don't think much of these flowers—they naturalize so vigorously they are sometimes considered weeds! In Ontario, where they aren't so easy to grow, lupines are prized for their colours and ability to attract hummingbirds and butterflies. While it seems that we often want what is the most difficult to grow in our gardens (like rhododendrons in Ottawa), fighting the natural climate or growing conditions in your region is not the best ecological way to go. (See Chapter 6 for more on plants that naturalize and naturalized landscapes.)

CREATE A XERISCAPE

Derived from *xeros*, the Greek word for "dry," this approach to gardening is all about using less water, and therefore making less work. Choosing drought-tolerant plants is key to a xeriscape, as is holding moisture in the soil via mulch, wind barriers and soil amendments. Watering systems such as soaker hoses and drip irrigation make the most of every drop. (See Chapter 15 for more on xeriscapes and water conservation and a list of drought-tolerant plants.)

GROUP PLANTS

Grouping plants with similar needs cuts down on the time and effort required to keep them looking good. For example, combine plants that need consistent moisture in an accessible spot close to your water source to make watering is quick and easy.

MULCH

Mulching is the best trick for creating a low-maintenance garden. In addition to holding moisture in the soil, it reduces the amount of weeding dramatically by preventing weed seeds from germinating. A good layer of mulch insulates the soil against temperature fluctuations. It allows the soil to warm up more quickly in the spring and protects the root systems from direct sunshine. (See Chapter 16 for everything you need to know about mulch.)

KEY ELEMENT

TRIPLE THE QUALITY!

Buy your triple mix from a reliable local supplier. I have seen many gardening projects with great potential fall flat on their faces due to poor soil. Keep in mind that the consistency of your soil should be that of chocolate cake—light, full of air (oxygen!) and somewhat sandy. If you're unsure where to go for quality soil, contact your local garden centre or Home Hardware for a recommendation.

Finely ground-up cedar mulch creates the perfect path.

While lawn isn't generally considered low-maintenance, I like to think of it as a sophisticated groundcover—a cool, green section of grass makes a pleasant visual break between beds and garden areas. Since many country gardens rely on well water as an irrigation source, and water conservation is crucial, choose hardy, drought-tolerant grass seed varieties. Don't worry if the lawn goes brown during dry spells; it almost inevitably bounces back when rain and cool temperatures return. The secret to lawn survival is to prepare the planting area well with a 10-centimetre (four-inch) layer of triple mix, which combines equal quantities of peat, compost and topsoil. (See Chapter 12 for more on lawn care.)

Perennial sunflower (Helianthus) covers a fence.

PICK TOUGH PLANTS

Anyone with a large garden is going to appreciate plants that don't require a lot of coddling. Look for plants that are not only drought-tolerant but also pest- and disease-resistant. Native plants have spent centuries adapting to our conditions and generally need far less fertilizing, watering and other maintenance than introduced exotics do. (See Chapter 6 for more on native plants.)

THE GARDENER'S WORK ROOM

With a big property, you have the luxury of creating a "work room"—ideally out of sight from the rest of the garden so you can walk away from the work without worrying about the appearance.

This space can be a holding area for plants you take out but want to relocate later when they have matured; a place to try out plants to see if you would like them in other areas of the garden; a spot to grow transplants and seedlings; and a storage area for garden supplies that don't need to be in the shed or barn. Bags of soil, stone, wooden skids and the like all need a place, preferably one that is handy but hidden. You can also use this area to build and store compost bins—you're sure to need more than one on a large country property.

A lattice-covered pergola provides a cool work area.

My "Taj - ma- compost" at Mary's Yarns, Unionville, Ontario.

A tool shed can be both decorative and functional.

BIN THERE, DONE THAT!

While visiting some of the great public gardens of Britain with my friend and garden personality Denis Flanagan, we were hosted by his brother John, a career gardener who lives in the south of England. While visiting one of his clients' gardens, I asked John where all the garden junk and compost was stored. He was very reluctant, but after much persuasion he showed me a compost bin, hidden at the back of the garden, that he had constructed only that summer. I think he looks like a proud poppa, don't you?

A COUNTRY GARDEN POND

When you have a large site, you have the luxury of installing sizeable garden features like ponds, big fountains and even mini-waterfalls.

An irrigation pond is a valuable addition to a extensive country property. This can be left natural or it can be the focus of a summer sitting area with a variety of furnishings including benches, tables, chairs and umbrellas. You can opt for larger sizes and a greater selection of furnishings on a generous site. You don't want them to "disappear" or look dwarfed by their surroundings. Similarly, don't skimp on the size of structures such as trellises, arbours, pergolas and gazebos, and elements such as fountains and statuary. Keep objects in scale—it is still possible to go too large and overpowering—and place them carefully for maximum effect. If your property is mostly in full sun, consider creating some areas of shade.

A country garden is the perfect setting for a pond.

Water Feature 2

RECIPES FOR RABBIT CONTROL

- Baby powder applied to young seedlings will make them unpalatable.
- Garlic powder on mature plants has a similar effect.
- Plant a large number of garlic plants around cherished plants to disguise the desirable scent.

COUNTRY GARDEN WILDLIFE

When you choose to live in a country setting, you are also choosing to live among a wide variety of wildlife. As experienced gardeners know, animals don't always see the same things in the lovely banks of flowers as we do. Of course, we share a more united approach to the vegetable patch—a great source of dinner—but this isn't any easier as we scramble to get to the beans before our four-legged friends do!

One country gardener told me of her mysteriously disappearing Asiatic lilies. Each day she would check on their progress, but invariably the buds that were promising to open would be completely missing before they had a chance to do so. She suspected deer had acquired a taste for her tender lilies. Their other favourite foods include impatiens, hostas, daylilies and stonecrops. Deer, along with rabbits and other small creatures, are also notorious for eating the bark off young trees in the winter and early spring.

There are ways to ward off these uninvited dinner guests. Young trees can be protected by covering their trunks with spiral plastic trunk protectors, hardware cloth or wire mesh. Flowers and vegetables are another

matter. A mesh fence 60 centimetres (two feet) high may keep out rabbits—and only then if you bury the fence at least 30 centimetres (one foot) underground. Deterring deer requires a fence at least two metres (six feet) high, but some deer can bound over even that with apparent ease. I recommend a fence that is three metres (nine feet) high, minimum. Such barriers may be the answer for a vegetable garden, but it's not likely that fences like these are part of your country garden vision. They are also not practical for protecting flower beds.

Bulbs can be protected from squirrels with a small square of loose nylon mesh or metal chicken wire placed over the bulbs and covered with earth. This should be removed in the spring if you are covering large bulbs. Squirrels aren't partial to blood meal, which can be dug into the soil when planting bulbs. However, raccoons may be attracted by the scent. There are good organic animal repellents in spray or solid form that are harmless to wildlife. These taste and scent repellents last for weeks and will effectively protect spring-flowering bulbs if sprayed on them at planting time.

ALL-PURPOSE REPELLENT RECIPE

Use 1 bulb garlic, 1 chopped onion, 2 tablespoons Tabasco, 2 tablespoons cayenne pepper, 2 drops oil, 1 tablespoon liquid soap and 1 litre water. Blend all ingredients and spray around plants for protection from most critters.

RECIPES FOR DEER REPELLENT

Of all the homemade rodent and deer repellents that I have heard of, the ones that seem to work most consistently contain rotten eggs. Here are two:

1. Mix 18 eggs in 20 litres (five gallons) of water and spray the solution over one acre. Deer, like people, dislike the stench of rotting eggs, but the solution is so dilute that humans can't detect the smell.

2. Mix 1 dozen eggs in a bucket with four cubes of beef bouillon. Fill the bucket with water and cover with a lid. Let this mixture sit until it has a strong odour. Add 2 tablespoons of liquid soap per gallon of liquid. Pour the completed mixture into a spray bottle and spray on plants. If you are using this recipe to protect a vegetable garden or edible crop, do not spray the mixture directly on the plant. Spray it around the plant as a protective barrier.

DEER-RESISTANT PLANTS

PERENNIALS	ZONE
Anise hyssop (*Agastache foeniculum*)	6
Aster (*Aster*)	5
Astilbe (*Astilbe*)	3
Beardtongue (*Penstemon*)	4
Bee balm (*Monarda didyma*)	3
Birdsfoot violet (*Viola pedata*)	3
Black-eyed Susan (*Rudbeckia hirta*)	5
Blanketflower (*Gaillardia*)	2
Bleeding heart (*Dicentra*)	2
Bloodroot (*Sanguinaria canadensis*)	3
Bluebell bellflower (*Campanula rotundifolia*)	2
Branched coneflower (*Rudbeckia triloba*)	4
Canada columbine (*Aquilegia canadensis*)	2

PERENNIALS	ZONE
Cardinal flower (*Lobelia cardinalis*)	4
Catmint (*Nepeta*)	4
Clematis (*Clematis*)	4
Daylily (*Hemerocallis*)	2
Delphinium (*Delphinium*)	4
False indigo (*Baptisia australis*)	4
False Solomon's seal (*Smilacina racemosa*)	3
Feather reed grass (*Calamagrostis* x *acutiflora*)	3
Fountain grass (*Pennisetum*)	6
Foxglove (*Digitalis*)	4
Globe thistle (*Echinops ritro*)	2
Goldenrod (*Solidago* hybrids)	2
Japanese anemone (*Anemone* x *hybrida*)	5
Joe-Pye weed (*Eupatorium maculatum*)	4
Lily of the valley (*Convallaria majalis*)	3

PERENNIALS	ZONE
Lupine (*Lupinus*)	3
Meadowsweet (*Filipendula*)	3
Monkshood (*Aconitum*)	2
Nodding wild onion (*Allium cernuum*)	2
Painted fern (*Athyrium*)	6
Pale purple coneflower (*Echinacea pallida*)	4
Peony (*Paeonia*)	4
Purple coneflower (*Echinacea purpurea*)	3
Shasta daisy (*Leucanthemum* x *superbum*)	4
Snow-in-summer (*Cerastium tomentosum*)	1
Spurge (*Euphorbia*)	6
Thyme (*Thymus*)	4
Wormwood (*Artemisia*)	2
Yarrow (*Achillea*)	3

SHRUBS	ZONE
'Anthony Waterer' spirea (*Spiraea* x *bumalda*)	4
Barberry (*Berberis*)	4
Bearberry cotoneaster (*Cotoneaster dammeri*)	5
Beautybush (*Kolkwitzia amabilis*)	5
'Blue Star' juniper (*Juniperus squamata*)	4

SHRUBS	ZONE
Bridal wreath spirea (*Spiraea prunifolia*)	4
Cinquefoil (*Potentilla fruticosa*)	3
Butterfly bush (*Buddleja*)	5
Lilac (*Syringa vulgaris*)	4
Currant (*Ribes*)	5

SHRUBS	ZONE
English holly (*Ilex aquifolium*)	6
Firethorn (*Pyracantha coccinea*)	5
Forsythia (*Forsythia* x *intermedia*)	5
Mugo pine (*Pinus mugo*)	2
Red osier dogwood (*Cornus sericea*)	2
Red twig dogwood (*Cornus alba*)	3

TREES	ZONE
Allegheny serviceberry (*Amelanchier laevis*)	5
Austrian pine (*Pinus nigra*)	4
Colorado blue spruce (*Picea pungens*)	2

TREES	ZONE
Flowering quince (*Chaenomeles speciosa*)	5
Dwarf Alberta spruce (*Picea glauca* 'Conica')	2
Eastern red cedar (*Juniperus virginiana*)	4

TREES	ZONE
Eastern white pine (*Pinus strobus*)	3
Honey locust (*Gleditsia triacanthos*)	4
Japanese maple (*Acer palmatum*)	5

A praying mantis, one of the good guys.

Some people swear by home-made preparations such as bags of human hair trimmings or soap scraps suspended near plants and trees to repel deer. If the animals around your country property are hungry enough, they are not likely to be deterred by these. For areas close to the home, consider installing an outdoor light with a motion detector. The light will scare away most of your nocturnal visitors, until they get used to it.

Take note of the specific plants that are eaten each year by unwanted visitors. As you begin to replace these plants, you will know what to avoid planting. However, if this trial-and-error approach is too time-consuming, costly and frustrating, you can try planting your ornamental gardens so

Dragonflies love to eat mosquitoes.

densely that a few green, flowerless stalks are more likely to go unnoticed.

As far as squirrels go - the most persistent pest of them all and perhaps the greatest in numbers coast to coast—I believe they are smarter than we are. After you have done all that you can think of or had recommended to you to get them out and keep them out of your yard and birdseed, perhaps the best approach is to accept them as our neighbours. Nuisances that they are, life is too short to get too upset by them.

Remember, some gardeners spend a great deal of time and effort creating gardens to attract wildlife. Why not sit back with a pair of binoculars for evening or early morning observation?

GOOD GUYS

There are some advantages to welcoming wildlife to your garden. Ladybugs devour aphids, mealybugs, scale and spider mites. Praying mantises help control the population of leaf hoppers and leaf-eating insects. Praying mantis egg cases can be purchased in June and placed in the garden. Dragonflies are a welcome addition to any garden as they have a healthy appetite for mosquitoes. Bees are well known for their hard work as pollinators and most experienced gardeners encourage their presence. Wasps, however, have gained the reputation as a nuisance in the garden. Before you invest in a wasp trap, consider the fact that wasps feed on leaf-eating worms and are a valuable part of insect control in the garden.

WASP CONTROL RECIPE

If wasps do become a problem, try this: Mix 1 can of (cheap) tuna with 1 tablespoon abrasive cleanser, 1 teaspoon vegetable oil. Place as near the source of the problem as possible. Wasps are attracted to the tuna, take it to the nest and the colony is wiped out. Take the mixture in at night, when raccoons can be drawn to it, and ***keep it away from cats!***

Toads can consume thousands of insects in vegetable gardens and

Daisy-type flowers attract many kinds of pollinators.

ornamental gardens. Encourage toads into your gardens by providing cool, moist and sheltered environments.

Snakes are feared by many but they should be celebrated for their many benefits. They eat rodents and some insects. They don't damage the garden by chewing or digging as they move among the plants. With rare exceptions, snakes are non-aggressive creatures and will not bite unless stepped on or threatened with injury.

Creating a beautiful garden in the country, above all, is an undertaking that needs to develop over time. Create a time line for your garden plan that extends out for at least three years: watch the garden evolve, note your own inclinations to visit certain parts of it over others and observe how your guests react to it. All this will offer you clues on how to proceed to the next step in the development of your country garden. In my experience, it is satisfying and fun.

Joe-Pye weed, grasses and false sunflowers create a natural-looking landscape.

CHAPTER SIX
Native Plant Gardening

As I travel across the country talking to Canadians about their gardens, I find that an increasing number of gardeners are turning to native plants and naturalized gardens. Looking for something "new," some gardeners are bypassing recent cultivars of popular ornamentals for the native introductions to the nursery trade. Some want a completely different look for their gardens—a natural-looking meadow, for example, rather than formally designed flower beds.

Others are taking an interest in native plants as an aspect of our natural heritage.

Fact is, you do not have to restrict the use of native plants to the informal, blowsy style of gardens that we associate with wildflowers. Often a native plant fits very nicely into a more formally designed garden. By definition, native plants are those that grew here naturally before the Europeans arrived. Indeed, anyone interested in Canadian history should be interested in this land that we have inhabited and call our own. Above all, native plants offer a host of practical advantages for the Canadian gardener.

WHY GO NATIVE?

Native plants have evolved here in North America over thousands of years. Competing for their very existence, they have adapted to their environment, making them easy to grow, particularly when garden conditions are similar to their native habitat.

Tolerating local growing conditions without (much) effort from us humans, they provide habitat for a variety of wildlife. Migrating butterflies, hummingbirds, songbirds and a host of pollinators can find native plants very attractive!

Most have few water demands and tend to be remarkably resistant to disease and insects, eliminating the need for pest or disease control. You could say that Mother Nature has preconditioned native plants to the vagaries of disease and insects down through many generations.

As an organic gardener, I have been attracted to native plants and, since moving to the country, I now have endless possibilities for native plants in my landscape.

WHAT IS A REAL NATIVE?

"Native" is a relative term: what is indigenous to one area of Canada is not necessarily indigenous to another. The popular purple coneflower (*Echinacea purpurea*) is native to the Canadian prairies. It grows very well in many parts of Canada, including my Ontario garden, but I cannot truly claim it to be native—not to my region anyhow. Wildflowers are those that grow without cultivation but they are not necessarily native. Many

Purple cone flower (Echinacea purpurea) is a Canadian prairie native.

European imports have found Canadian soil to their liking and have spread far and wide on their own. Dandelions, Queen Anne's lace and field daisies are just a few of these newcomers.

NATIVE VS. NATURALIZED

Today, many people talk about "naturalized" gardens, but they aren't necessarily talking about the same thing. Native plant enthusiasts and environmentalists refer to an approach that attempts to return a local landscape to its pre-agricultural, pre-settler state: in other words, an area is being planted exclusively with species native to that region or micro—region, creating a balanced ecosystem. When you see civic naturalization projects in parks, schoolyards and empty lots, this is generally what is being done.

More familiar is using the word "naturalizing" in reference to plants like bulbs. In this sense, naturalized is referring to a plant behaviour—after being planted in a random way, they are allowed to multiply and spread of their own accord. In the fall, look for bulbs sold as "suitable for naturalizing" if you are seeking to create spreading carpets of spring colour.

A plant that lends itself to "naturalizing" will make itself at home in your garden. It will grow and thrive over many years. But it is not necessarily "native"!

These daffodils aren't native but have naturalized.

False sunflower (Heliopsis)

To some gardeners and gardening writers, the naturalized garden is similar to what I like to call the low-maintenance garden. This involves planting only what thrives in your garden conditions (no extraordinary measures, no fertilizing, and little if any watering after the plants are established). It also involves using plant material that spreads while being ignored by the gardener. You allow those plants to find their own space in your garden, competing with other species until a balance is struck and a stable ecosystem is established.

CREATING A NATURALIZED LOOK

Plants suitable for naturalizing spread and shift, which means that the garden style is natural and unscripted in appearance. Borders and distinct groupings of plants give way to a fluid, ever-changing landscape. In this approach, native and hardy perennials are preferred over annuals. However, if you are planning to grow a native garden in the strictest sense of it, you will use native plants exclusively.

Native plants also provide a connection to surrounding natural areas. By planting native plants, you are supporting local biodiversity (meaning the range and variety of different species and habitats in an area) and you are not introducing alien species. Many alien plants have also adapted (very quickly) to our environment, and since some of these invasive introductions have no natural predators here, they can out-compete the natives. If you have aggressive exotic plants in your garden, make sure they don't overrun the native plants. Also, weed your garden well until the native plants become established, which can take three to five years.

While there are many native plants that nurseries and gardeners have known and loved for years, there are many other Canadian native plants that have never been grown by gardeners.

Prairie blazingstar (Liatrus) mingles beautifully with tall grasses.

I don't use native plants exclusively, but they dominate my butterfly garden much of the year.

DISCOVERING THE PAST

How do you determine what is native to your area? Canada is an enormous geographical expanse that spans 10 provinces and three territories. There are more than 13,000 gorgeous native plants from which to choose for the garden. According to the Go For Green Program, the number of native plants in each province are:

British Columbia:	2,170
Alberta:	1,600
Saskatchewan:	1,180
Manitoba:	1,290
Ontario:	1,930
Quebec:	1,810
New Brunswick:	970
Nova Scotia:	1,030
Prince Edward Island:	640
Newfoundland:	820

(www.goforgreen.ca/gardening)

Within each province and territory, there are bioregions—geographic areas having common characteristics of soil, climate and native plants (many unique to that particular biore-gion). To discover what your area might have been like before it was cleared for agriculture or housing and what plants are native to your region, check the following resources:

• The North American Native Plant Society (www.nanps.org).

• Wildflower books or field guides that list what plants are native to a particular area.

• If your local garden centre carries native plants, ask which bioregion they came from.

• *Grow Wild! Native Plant Gardening in Canada*, by Lorraine Johnson (Toronto: Random House, 1998).

• Your local conservation authority:
  www.conservancy.bc.ca,
  www.ab-conservation.com
  www.natureconservancy.ca
  www.gov.mb.ca/conservation
  www.trca.on.ca,www.svca.on.ca
  www.natureconservancy.ca

• My website,www.markcullen.com, also has information on native plants and links to other helpful sites and organizations.

Keep in mind that you must also judge what native plants will work in your garden or what bioregion your property mimics. Perhaps at one point your backyard was part of a savannah, but now it is filled with succulent vegetation and shade trees. The soil may have been amended every year, trees have been planted and efficient watering systems are in place. Would returning it to a grasslands-like garden or a native meadow garden work or seem appropriate? Perhaps native woodland plants are a better choice.

If you live in a newer neighbourhood, chances are that your soil is very poor (as all the good stuff was stripped away for construction). In that case, a meadow-like garden with tough native plants may be the solution. That, unfortunately, is the state of 'developer's top soil'.

The other important factor to remember is that you don't have to create a garden of exclusively native plants. While some gardeners are interested in creating a wholly native ecosystem on their property, in my experience, most gardeners combine native plants with others to create more traditional or formal garden designs. Even from an environmental standpoint, your use of native plants doesn't have to be an all-or-nothing decision. "The Benefits of Growing Native Plants," a helpful pamphlet published by the Toronto Parks and Recreation department and the High Park Citizen's Advisory committee, notes that "if each gardener replaces just two invasive alien species with native plants, the results will be significant." Go to www.highpark.org for more information.

NATIVE WOODLAND PLANTS AND GARDENS

Whether creating an entire woodland garden or using woodland native plants, you must have similar conditions to their natural homes. Remember that the most pervasive colour in the woods is green—many woodland plants feature wonderfully textured and shaped foliage rather than vibrant flowers. Canadian wild ginger, for example, has a lovely, deep green, heart-shaped leaf that more than makes up for its rather quiet rusty-brown blooms.

Some woodland denizens are spring "ephemerals," which means that, after their early burst of colourful flowering, they go dormant.

By all means, include some of these in your garden, but make sure you have other summer plants that will grow in to disguise the bare spots left by the ephemerals.

The majority of woodland plants flower in spring when they receive sun or dappled sun before the leaves are out on the trees. They spend the rest of the growing season in the shade of the tree canopy so they won't thrive or survive in full summer sun. Woodland plants enjoy the friable, humusy, slightly acidic soil created by decomposing leaves. A layer at least 12 centimetres (five inches) deep of leaf mould is essential when planting a woodland garden.

Even if you are starting with good soil, you will want to mimic nature and add a layer of organic matter at least once a year (this is a good gardening practice with non-native plants, too). This is the best excuse you'll find anywhere for leaving your fallen leaves on the surface of the soil. If you do not have an adequate supply in your own yard, "borrow" them from neighbours! A spring application of compost, well-rotted manure or leaf mould, and a winter mulch of chopped leaves are ideal.

Nodding wild onion (Allium cernuum).

Greens Superintendent Larry Allen's meadow. Meadow Brook Golf and Country Club, Gormley, Ontario.

THE RHYTHM OF THE MEADOW

Many people imagine a wildflower meadow to be a field dominated by colour with poppies in full bloom, fragrance and bird song. It is not, well, most of the time. While you may get lots of bird song throughout the gardening season, the period of intense blooming—and therefore colour—is remarkably short. Early in spring you may get a rush of low-growing plants in bloom and later in the summer the black-eyed Susans and purple coneflowers will provide a show. It is the grasses with their delicate seedheads and arching leaves that provide the rhythm of the meadow garden.

PRAIRIE AND MEADOW GARDENS

The Prairies are also commonly called grasslands where grasses predominate. Although most have

been lost to agriculture and development, there are three types of grasslands: the tall-grass prairie, which occurs in southwestern Ontario and southern Manitoba; the mixed-grass prairie in the southern parts of all three Prairie provinces; and the short-grass prairie, which characterizes the drier regions of Alberta and Saskatchewan. Other grassland landscapes, like oak savannahs, often bordered the prairies and the plains of the Midwest. But even if you live in an area that was once home to grasslands, re-establishing a prairie in your backyard is not likely to be an option, unless you have a

vast tract of open land and a great deal of time at your disposal (a prairie habitat would take several years to establish). What most gardeners are in fact attracted to is the idea of a meadow.

A meadow is a transitional ecosystem rather than a stable, self-perpetuating landscape like a prairie. Meadows develop in areas where tree cover has been disturbed or removed, providing a sunny site, often surrounded by the original woodlands. Here grasses, forbs (herbs other than grasses) and wildflowers thrive until the shrubs and trees succeed them to cover the land.

True meadows are not, as you might assume, low-maintenance gardens, at least not initially. Many of the plants are slow to establish and are easy prey to weeds that will choke them out. What's more, meadow plants thrive in the same conditions as many weeds or invasive non-natives - disturbed, loose soil and full sun. To allow meadow plants to gain a foothold, the site must be prepared well to kill existing weed seeds in the soil. Rototill the earth at least one full season before planting. Cover it with heavy black plastic to kill weed seeds. The black plastic will have to remain on the soil for at least six weeks in the heat of early summer to really "cook" the weed seeds below.

KEY ELEMENT

A FATHER'S DAY MOWING

For the first three years of your meadow's life, an annual mowing is very important. Set your mower height at it highest and, above all, mow after the first flush of early spring growth has matured and before it goes to seed. This mowing helps to get the dreaded burdock and Canada thistle under control and gives the more desirable flowering plants a chance to grow later in June and early July. For most regions in Canada, this should occur between June 15 and 30.

The growing number of Canadians using native plants in their landscapes tells me that this is an idea whose time has definitely come. More than just a nod to patriotism or our natural history, using native plants has many benefits. Try a few and, in time, I'll bet you will be hooked!

Once the soil is prepared, the meadow must be hand-weeded aggressively for the first two years. What's more, to create a true meadow and help it thrive, you must use a mix of native grasses (at least 50 per cent) as well as native flowering plants. The grasses not only provide structural support for the flowers, but as they grow, they also cover the surface of the soil, leaving less space for weeds to get a foothold. The grasses will establish their roots just below the surface, out-competing the weeds' roots. (Wildflowers offer less competition because they send their roots much deeper.)

Once meadows are established, they need little attention, other than mowing to a height of 10 to 15 centimetres (four to six inches) once a year. This shearing replicates the fires or grazing and trampling by animals that keep native grasses and flowers strong while reducing weeds and woody growth that would overcome them. I have found that the best time to cut my meadow down is in mid June — around Father's Day.

Keep in mind that it is still a transitional ecosystem—plants are likely to spread themselves about and naturalize, changing the appearance of the garden every year. True meadows are a delightful landscape—delicate and subtle in colouring, and ever-shifting in pattern and texture. If a meadow is appropriate to your site, the initial labour may be worth it. Before embarking, however, read more about meadow gardening (I have information on my website, www.markcullen.com) or consult a Canadian meadow-gardening specialist such as Wildflower Farm (www.wildflowerfarm.com) or Sweet Grass Gardens (www.sweetgrassgardens.com).

Even if you don't install a true meadow, you can still use native plants to create a meadow-type garden that conforms more easily to the space, time and practices of an urban or suburban gardener. Over the last few years, many native meadow or prairie flowers have become increasingly popular at the garden centres—sun-lovers like black-eyed Susans, purple coneflowers, obedient plant and butterfly weed are being embraced for their drought-tolerance, hardiness and pest-resistance as well as their gorgeous petals.

Grey-headed coneflowers(Ratibida pinnata).

Big bluestem.

Butterfly weed.

Little bluestem.

MY FAVOURITE NATIVE MEADOW PLANTS

Aster (*Aster*)	Zone 3
Big bluestem (*Andropogon gerardii*)	Zone 3
Black-eyed Susan (*Rudbeckia hirta*)	Zone 3
Blue grama grass (*Bouteloua gracilis*)	Zone 3
Butterfly weed (*Asclepias tuberosa*)	Zone 4
Coreopsis (*Coreopsis grandiflora*)	Zone 4
Evening primrose (*Oenothera*)	Zone 3
False indigo (*Amorpha fruticosa*)	Zone 3
Goldenrod (*Solidago*)	Zone 3
Grey-headed coneflower (*Ratibida pinnata*)	Zone 3
Little bluestem (*Schizachyrium scoparium*)	Zone 3
Prairie blazingstar (*Liatris pycnostachya*)	Zone 3
Purple prairie clover (*Petalostemum purpureum*)	Zone 3
Switch grass (*Panicum virgatum*)	Zone 4
Wild bergamot (*Monarda fistulosa*)	Zone 3

New England aster.

Goldenrod.

A gorgeous cottage garden has its own challenges.

CHAPTER SEVEN
The Cottage Garden

In most gardening literature, "cottage garden" refers to a style of garden, specifically the English cottage garden look. When Canadian gardeners hear the word, "cottage," they tend to think of a place in the woods by a lake, where summer days are spent away from urban life. Here, I am referring to the cottage garden in terms of the latter definition—a place where we encounter entirely different challenges from those we face in our city gardens.

And, of course, this chapter is also useful to anyone who lives in cottage country permanently.

Gardening at the cottage means that you are likely to be gardening in a growing zone that you're not used to, with a markedly different soil structure from that in your town garden. You will probably have to deal with heavy shade from mature trees, and you will also have many more insects and four-legged visitors to your flower beds. Above all, you must think about how to manage a garden that you are not there to maintain on a regular basis. But before you make your first planting, think about what you really want from your cottage landscape.

SET PRIORITIES

Take a look around your cottage property. Perhaps you just want to enhance the natural environment or, at the other extreme, completely morph your yard into something very beautiful and personal.

Trees surround a casual walkway at a cottage.

What do you like about the existing landscape? What would you like to change? If you are just starting on a garden plan for your cottage, I suggest that you consider extending the landscape theme that has already been established by Mother Nature herself to create a seamless, naturalistic look. Or maybe you are hankering for a splash of colour to contrast with the native greenery and the blues of the sky and water.

Once you have determined your gardening design goal, spend a little time thinking about how you might achieve it. If you find yourself coming up with ideas you've used or have noticed in urban settings, ask yourself if these solutions are appropriate for your cottage. After all, a cottage is an ideal place to try something a little different.

Picture yourself—and be realistic about how much gardening time you'll have.

GROWING CONDITIONS

Pay close attention to the light levels in the areas you want to plant. Many cottages are set in relatively dense shade or dappled sunlight at best, with very few spots that get the minimum six hours of sunlight needed for sun-loving plants. In addition, the shade is probably caused not by buildings, but rather by trees, which also take most of the moisture from the soil. So plants that cope with dry shade will be at the top of your list.

KEY ELEMENT

PICK EASY-CARE PLANTS

As you develop your cottage garden, choose hardy, pest-resistant plants that can tolerate some neglect and a fairly wide range of temperatures. Select plants that do not require much deadheading, like daylilies, hostas, bergenias, peonies and many ornamental grasses. Use low-maintenance groundcovers such as Japanese spurge and Canadian wild ginger, shrubs such as button bush and winterberry, and, if you have shade, ferns and Solomon's seal.

ASSESS AVAILABLE TIME

Next, ask yourself how much time you really want to spend gardening at the cottage. Most people will say that they really don't want to garden much at all —sailing, swimming or simply relaxing with a good book may be more appealing. If gardening is your hobby and, like me, you find it a great way to relax, you must still be realistic about how much time you will be spending at the cottage and how much of that time will be available for gardening.

Unless you are one of those lucky people who can move lock, stock and barrel to your cottage for the entire summer, you likely must be satisfied with a week or two here and there and as many weekends as you can cram in during the warm months. If you really adore getting your hands into the earth, that may mean spending your whole weekend gardening like mad, doing as much weeding and watering, pruning and deadheading as you can. Or it could mean creating gardens that thrive on neglect, requiring only minimal attention to stay healthy and beautiful.

PLAN YOUR COLOUR

A third consideration when planning your garden should be assessing when you spend the most time at the cottage. If, for example, you take your longest vacation at the end of the summer, you will want to plant late-blooming flowers. Why bother putting in a glorious bed of irises when you will be gazing at spent, flowerless stalks for your two weeks' holiday in August?

RAISED BEDS OR GARDEN BEDS?

Our big country provides a huge variety of soil conditions in cottage country. If your soil is challenging, you can amend the soil in your garden beds, but if you are putting in a new garden or expanding an existing one, it will be easier and more effective in the long run to simply replace existing soil.

Another option is to create raised beds. These provide better drainage than garden beds, give you complete control over the quality of the soil you grow in and can help you avoid the problem of competing tree roots.

If you don't want raised beds and you want to keep the soil that is there natu-

Purple wintercreeper (Euonymus fortunei 'coloratus') is a tough, shade-tolerant, woody groundcover.

rally, you will have to break up the existing topsoil, removing rocks or clay if necessary, and add very generous quantities of finished compost or composted cattle or steer manure. By "gen-

The understory in a heavily treed garden.

erous," I mean a layer no less than eight centimetres (three inches) deep.

It is important to understand your soil's pH level (how acidic or alkaline it is) by testing with a simple, inexpensive soil test kit. While most gardening experts agree that the fallen needles from a few pine trees on an urban lot are not going to have much effect on the acidity of soil, the soil in a coniferous forest is a different story.

If the humus in your area is made up primarily of decaying spruce needles, you'll likely have quite acidic soil (spruce needles tend to be the most acidic, with pine and fir less so). Save yourself a lot of grief by choosing plants that thrive in the pH range you have, rather than fighting it by using plants that have naturally opposite requirements. (See Chapter 13 for more about soil types, pH and amendments.)

NATIVE PLANTS

Native plant gardening is a natural fit for the cottage garden. What better way to ensure success than by using flower, tree and shrub species that are already growing naturally around your cottage? Not only will your landscaping

blend in seamlessly with the surrounding area, but your plantings will also have the best possible chance of surviving.

While it often takes some research to figure out what plants might have originally been native to your urban lot, discovering the native state of your cottage land should be downright easy. Wander through the surrounding woods and fields and make a list of what you see growing there. Better still, take photographs of the plants that you like the look of, including the bloom, if possible.

Many garden centres now sell native plants that are nursery-grown. Show a Certified Horticultural Technician either your plant list or photos and you will be on your way to discovering a whole new family of plants that are suitable for growing in your region. (See Chapter 6 for more on native plants.)

INVASIVE PLANTS

Avoid planting invasive plants at your cottage. In a city or suburban garden, there are plenty of constraints on a plant's ability to travel. Your lawn and its regular mowing, the sidewalks,

Variegated goutweed (Aegopodium podagraria) is extremely aggressive and can overrun native plants if let loose.

house foundations, roads and so on are natural barriers to a plant's spreading habit. What's more, plants that result from seeds that travel via the wind (or birds) to your neighbour's gardens and lawns are likely to meet the weed-picker's hands if they are not wanted. There are few such restraints at most cottages where the garden, whether extensively landscaped or not, tends to blend into the surrounding terrain. Plants that like the conditions that they are growing in can spread and multiply much more aggressively than they might in the city.

While hiking the Bruce Trail in Ontario one summer, I came across an extensive patch of periwinkle (*Vinca minor*) that must have once been planted as a groundcover around an old farmhouse. The house was long gone, but the periwinkle persisted—not only had it spread out under native pine trees but it was also creeping along the roadside for a considerable distance and had travelled well into the bush. Yes, it was a beautiful green carpet under the trees, but what native plants had it choked out? What essential elements of this forest's natural understory were now missing?

When we plant non-native plants around our cottage properties, I think that we have an ecological responsi-

bility to ensure we are not introducing problem plants to the woods and fields around us.

Be especially cautious about planting anything that is very quick-growing. Avoid groundcovers like periwinkle and goutweed (*Aegopodium podagraria*), one of the most pernicious plants known. Beware of invasive perennials such as creeping bellflower (*Campanula rapunculoides*) and now-storied purple loosestrife (*Lythrum salicaria*), and resist aggressive woody plants like silver lace vine, Manitoba maple, Norway maple, Oriental bittersweet, willow and red twig dogwood
.

For a detailed list of invasive plants found in Canada, check out the Canadian Botanical Conservation Network, which identifies plants in three categories:

Trees, shrubs/vines and herbaceous species (www.rbg.ca/cbcn/en).

ROCKS

If your cottage is set among rocky outcroppings in a sunny location, take advantage of it by using some of this rock as the basis for a rock garden, if you have time and the inclination. Rocks can be useful if you are attempting to maintain soil on a slope, so you might consider moving some of them around your property to create new rocky outcroppings.

Plant colourful annuals at the cottage if you're going to be there to enjoy them.

GO BIG

When planning a cottage garden, keep the larger scale in mind. Most cottages are surrounded by big trees and/or big rocks so small-scale plantings might be lost. To compete with the larger landscape and give your garden authority, plant fewer types of flowers but in greater numbers for generous drifts of colour.

THE QUESTION OF GRASS

Even if you decide to confine your ornamental gardening to your city garden, there is always the question of what to do with the grounds surrounding the cottage. If the cottage is set on rocks or close to the woodlands, you may just let nature take its course. But many cottages are set in clearings of various sizes. If it is a large clearing, creating a native meadow on all or portions of it may be the answer.

Meadows are actually a transition stage in the development of woodland that naturally occurs after the land has been cleared. It is a wonderfully logical solution to open space around a cottage. Meadows take a number of years to establish, so they are not low-maintenance at first. They also require periodic mowing and other maintenance to ensure they don't revert to

A lawn might be tempting at the cottage but keep the mowing in mind.

Moss and stone are a natural combination.

woodlands (See Chapter 6 for details on making meadows.)

Some people might look at the clearing around their cottage and start picturing a lush suburban lawn there. However, this lawn probably won't get the kind of regular upkeep your city lawn demands and receives. To my way of thinking, mowing the lawn and cottage life do not go hand in hand. Why interrupt the wonderful sound of bird song and breezes blowing through the trees with the roar of a motor?

A mulched perennial garden needs less weeding and watering.

A way of protecting seeds and seedlings is cheesecloth (a natural cotton fabric) or a floating row cover (a sheet of white spun-bond poly-ester). Sold in hardware stores or available from mail order gardening companies, both are open-weave fabrics that allow sunlight and rain through while preventing the soil from drying out—or at least slowing the process. You may have to resign yourself to losing a few plants if you aren't able to get to the cottage for a week or so during the critical germination period.

And even if you have the time and the inclination to mow your lawn regularly, you may not want to strain your well or pump with lawn watering. You might therefore consider planting attractive native groundcovers such as wild strawberry and bearberry.

If you have small children or are partial to badminton or croquet, you will need a groundcover that can tolerate a good deal of foot traffic, which brings us back to lawn. When shopping for grass seed for the cottage, you want something that is hardy, slow-growing, low-growing, drought-tolerant and can be walked and played on.

Black wood chip mulch

A rain barrel provides warm, oxegen-rich water.

Look for mixtures that include named varieties of creeping red fescue (*Festuca rubra*), chewings fescue (*F. r.* var. *commutata*) and hard fescue (*F. ovina* var. *duriuscula*). Fescues in general are tough, no-fuss grasses, but, because they are bunch grasses, they tend to create a bumpy lawn, so choose new cultivars that have less of a clump-forming habit. Drought-tolerant and slow-growing Canada bluegrass (*Poa compressa*) is also available in less clumpy cultivars.

Avoid mixtures that contain a high proportion of fast-growing grasses like Kentucky bluegrass (*Poa pratensis*) and perennial ryegrass (*Lolium perenne*) as they need frequent mowing and tend to dry out quickly. Don't forget that good preparation is the key to success for any type of lawn. (See Chapter 12 for more on lawns and lawn care.)

CARING FOR THE COTTAGE GARDEN

Even if you are an avid gardener, it's a good idea—for you and the environment—to make your cottage garden as easy-care as possible. Many of the ecologically friendly techniques that work in your home garden can be used at the cottage to save you time and effort.

New plantings can be a challenge because you may not be there for an extended period, and even hardy, drought-tolerant plants need frequent watering before they are established. The best bet is to get a neighbour to visit your garden during the week and water for you.

You can help the process (and save yourself work down the road) by using the gardener's secret weapon: mulch. As in every garden, a five- to eight-centimetre (two- to three-inch) deep layer of mulch is invaluable for holding moisture in the soil, and preventing

KEY ELEMENT

USE RAIN BARRELS
Make the most of every drop of water by installing rain barrels to collect water from your roof and eavestroughs. This will take some of the pressure off your well water supply.

Don't forget to compost at the cottage. You may not be putting vast quantities of kitchen scraps into your cottage composter but yard waste can add up quickly. Added to the composter, leaves and debris from around your cottage will provide much-needed carbon as a counterbalance to the nitrogen from kitchen scraps. If you are careful not to add meat or cooked foods, most animals will generally ignore the compost bin.

evaporation from sun and wind. My favourite mulch is finely ground pine or cedar bark. However, there are many other mulching materials including coco bean husks, finished compost and, of course, Mother Nature's own mulch and the one you might have the best access to at the cottage—fallen leaves. (See Chapter 17 for more on mulch.)

REDUCE WATERING

Gardening with less water is part of the organic gardener's mantra, and is even more crucial at the cottage where the water supply—and the time to spend watering—may be limited. Using hardy, drought-tolerant plants and water-wise practices is all part of the approach called xeriscaping. Tailor-made for cottage life, a xeriscape just takes some careful planning and a bit of research.

Not having to spend hours watering the garden every time you visit the cottage is an enormous time-saver. It also means less pruning because plants that are not over-watered or

over-fertilized require less paring back. And you'll have less weeding since, with less water and lots of mulch, you'll have fewer weeds. You won't have to worry so much about pests and diseases either because drought-tolerant plants tend to have less of the tender new growth that appeals to critters, and native plants attract lots of beneficial insects that will do the pest control for you. (See Chapter 15 for more on xeriscaping and water conservation.)

WILDLIFE IN THE COTTAGE GARDEN

Growing a garden in a woodland setting means dealing with wildlife, from rabbits and raccoons to skunks and squirrels and, of course, deer. Fencing is the most effective control but not always desirable or feasible. Besides physical barriers, there are various scare tactics and homemade recipes for sprays and repellents. Even though deer can't read the lists and a really hungry deer will eat just about anything, there are certainly plants that they tend to leave alone—particularly ones with aromatic, hairy or leathery foliage. (See Chapter 5 for a list of deer-resistant plants and more about wildlife control.)

ONE FOR YOU, TWO FOR ME!

Animals are part and parcel of the natural setting, which is why you go to

the cottage in the first place, so you might want to follow the approach taken by a caller to my radio show.

She recounted how she planted a small vegetable patch behind her cottage, and the first year everything came up splendidly. However, just before she was about to harvest her first taste of Swiss chard, she discovered that every last leaf had been mown down, apparently by some animal. The leaf lettuce, the radishes, the beans and the carrots had been left untouched.

She constructed a mesh fence 60 centimetres (two feet) high around her garden and planted another crop of chard, only to wake up early one morning to the sight of a hare leaping over the fence with a belly full of greens. The following year she gave up planting chard, and the disgruntled hare ravaged her lettuce instead.

From then on, she faithfully planted the chard—for the hare. That way, she figured, she could count on enjoying her lettuce and other vegetables. Sounds like good advice.

Gardening at the cottage may sound like a contradiction in terms, but for many of us, it sounds like another good reason to get out to the cottage—to relax and enjoy ourselves in a way that we really cannot or just do not while at home.

Sunflowers shine brightly in northern gardens.

CHAPTER EIGHT
The Northern Garden

Many people will say that gardening in Canada is gardening in the north.

But they do not live here.

"Gardening in the north" in this book refers to locations in hardiness zones 2, 3 and 4. See the hardiness zone map on page 200 to determine your growing zone (and Chapter 1 for more about what these zones mean). Our northern land offers some stun-

Tree peonies on the prairies.

ning beauty but, for gardeners, its short growing season can be challenging. However, with a little ingenuity, experimentation and knowledge, it is possible to create a wonderful garden.

With a short growing season, it is important to keep in mind factors that can extend it, like the composition of your soil. Sandy soil heats up faster in spring and holds heat longer than clay soil, which works in quite the opposite way, taking much longer to warm up. A neighbour with sandy loam may see their perennials poke up through the ground a couple of weeks before your clay-based soil shows any evidence of life. If you have clay soil and want to see your flowers earlier or give your vegetables enough time to ripen before the first frosts roll around, consider making a large-scale addition of sharp sand (note: not beach sand!).

Dig in plenty of compost, manure or other well-decomposed organic matter to create a loam that will warm up more quickly. (See Chapter 13 for more on soil and amendments.)

A scoop of sharp sand.

KEY ELEMENT

1. Long days. The tilt of the earth on its axis come late spring and summer gives the northern gardener a long day and lots of sunshine or, if you are a farmer, lots of "sunshine hours" relative to more southern neighbours. You may start planting later in the season but often your garden's performance catches up with southern gardens.

2. Warm days, cool nights. Many plants, including tomatoes, grow best with hot, sunny daytime temperatures and relatively cool nights. Flower fertilization often occurs more efficiently too.

3. Fewer pests. Ever notice that many pests referred to in U.S. and British gardening books are foreign to the north? When the winter temperature dips way down and the ground freezes, many garden pests are minimized or eliminated. Goodbye, Japanese beetle!

4. Ground frost. Frost that penetrates deep into the ground promotes biodiversity and microbial activity. Mean nothing to you? Don't worry–just take my word for it.

RAISED BEDS

Raised beds improve drainage and make it easier to introduce soil amendments or replace soil without heavy digging to remove existing earth. In northern gardens, they have the added benefit of warming up more quickly in spring than beds at ground level. Placed against south-facing walls or built with a southerly exposure, they warm up even faster and stay warmer longer.

On the down side, raised beds dry out quickly and will need more watering than ground-level beds. I recommend that you lay a soaker hose just beneath the surface of the soil to keep plants watered efficiently at the root zone. Don't fill raised beds with sandy soil unless you amend it heavily with generous quantities of organic material—as much as four parts compost and soil to one part sand.

Soaker hose on soil.

A whole garden of raised beds harnesses all of the benefits while providing order to the scheme.

MICROCLIMATES

In any growing zone, there will be many small areas where the climate is quite different from that of the surrounding terrain. These little zones within a zone are called "microclimates." They are, however, seldom identified on maps—after all, they can be as small as a few square feet or as big as a few square miles.

Microclimates are naturally created by differences in the local topography. Rocks, stone and paved areas retain heat and create a warmer climate in their direct vicinity. Cities are signifi-cantly warmer than the area around them due to the high concentration of concrete, pavement and buildings that all retain and release heat. What's more, a city's smog can trap heat and keep the warmer air close to the ground. Large bodies of water moderate temperatures, making the area surrounding them cooler in the summer and warmer in the winter.

The southern exposure of slopes (and your home garden) will be sunnier and warmer, the northern exposure shadier and therefore cooler. Microclimates can be as small as the patch of earth on the southeast side of a boulder, out of the prevailing westerly winds and in the warmest sun. You may find hot spots you can take advantage of to grow plants that are recommended for a zone or two higher than yours or are simply borderline for your zone.

Conversely, there could be dry, windy or low—lying areas where plants that grow well elsewhere in your garden might struggle. Identifying—nd creating–microclimates in your garden may solve some of your enduring gardening dilemmas.

'Origami' columbine (Aquilegia) produces stunning early-summer colour.

An evergreen windbreak saves up to 23% in heating costs.

TAKE TIME TO OBSERVE

To identify the microclimates in your yard, it may take a year or two of close observation and keeping track of light and moisture levels; wind, sun and shade patterns; frost differences; snow cover; and what thrives and what fails in various areas. Pay particular attention to identical plants located in different parts of your yard.

The hardy Canadian rose, 'David Thompson'.

They offer excellent indicators about differing microclimates.

Take note of the first and last plants to bloom or to poke their way through the soil, and watch for the following:

FROST POCKETS

Dips in terrain and low-lying areas can create pockets of cooler temperatures as cold air flows down to fill them. The north side of walls or dense hedges may also be significantly cooler spots. Use winter mulches of straw and shred-ded bark in frost pockets to protect your plants and avoid freeze/thaw cycles.

Hardy, deep-rooted plants have less chance of being damaged by these cycles. Thin hedges by removing mature growth with a green-wood buck saw to improve air circulation and allow the sun to reach the core of each plant.

WIND TUNNELS AND WINDBREAKS

Wind is always a challenge for both plants and gardeners. Windy areas may be significantly cooler and will certainly be drier as more moisture is lost to evaporation. Wind tunnels are places where the wind is forced through a narrow space, therefore picking up pressure and speed. This happens between houses, structures, fences or trees.

Be mindful when building garden structures that you don't create potential wind tunnels. If you have a site where the wind blows unimpeded, I recommend that you install a windbreak in the form of a fence, a hedge or a line or grouping of evergreen trees and shrubs.

Planting a windbreak of tall evergreens on the north and northwest side of your house to divert the coldest winds not only creates a microclimate for the many plants that thrive in the morning sun, out of the wind, but can also save you a lot on heating costs.

A Texas Agricultural Extension Service study compared exposed houses to ones landscaped with properly positioned evergreen windbreaks. The houses with windbreaks demonstrated energy savings of up to 23 per cent.

In addition, large deciduous trees planted on the south and west sides will shade the house in summer, reducing indoor temperatures by as much as four to five degrees Celsius, yet allow the rays of the sun in to warm it in winter. They will also protect your plants from the most intense afternoon sun. According to Colorado State University, these measures can reduce heating bills by as much as 25 per cent and cooling bills by 50 per cent or more (go to www.virtuousconsumer.com for more information on the energy-saving potential of plants).

ARID SPOTS

Areas of your garden may be significantly drier than others. If you have high ground, the leeside will be drier (the windward side is likely to get more rain). Also, it is dry under the eaves and soffit of your house, garage or shed, close to big hedges and under mature trees and conifers.

Mulch the dry areas of your garden with a five-centimetre (two-inch) layer of finely ground cedar or pine bark. Even a generous 10-centimetre (four-inch) layer of fallen leaves can help significantly in retaining needed moisture in the soil in these dry spots.

A well place shade tree can cool a house considerably.

HEAT TRAPS AND COOL SPOTS

In a sunny location, rocks, stones, pavement and brick walls absorb heat and radiate it, creating a warmer microclimate. Light-coloured walls of any composition will also reflect the sun and heat, as well as block the wind and reduce wind chill. Take advantage of these heat traps—or build a brick or stone wall to create one—to grow "hot-crop" vegetables such as peppers and tomatoes and other flowering annuals that will relish the extra warmth as it radiates off the wall. Plant some early spring-flowering bulbs, too—they will bloom much earlier.

If you do build a walled garden, make sure it faces south or southwest so it captures the most sun and warmth.

The brick or stone will radiate heat right through the cool of the evening and nighttime.

Conversely, if you identify cool spots in your garden, you can redesign them into heat traps, or simply choose plants that are hardy to one zone below your own to ensure success in those spots. For example, if your garden is Zone 3, put in a plant hardy to Zone 2.

Creating and using microclimates is a useful gardening approach with a long history going back to medieval times. The splendid walled gardens the Victorians built were not just an effort to gain privacy; they were also a brilliant way of creating a variety of microclimates within a single garden.

Handsome brick terraces that act as raised beds make good use of a steep slope.

Nature provides her own surprises, like this tree growing out of an expanse of rock.

Since alpines are small and need good drainage, a rock garden or a rocky slope are ideal settings for them. They can also be planted in the gaps of retaining walls, along stone or gravel paths, and even in containers or raised beds as long as you prepare the appropriate soil.

PLANTS AND PLANTING

ADMIRABLE ALPINES

Thriving on short summers with their long, relatively cool days, alpine plants are a terrific option for northern gardens. Many are native to the Arctic tundra and high mountain altitudes, often above the timberline.

Most alpine plants are compact perennials that grow low to withstand the weight of winter snow cover and protect themselves from strong winds the rest of the year. Growing close to the ground also ensures that they remain where it is warmest–next to the soil that absorbs and reflects the heat of the sun. Many of these plants are also evergreen—they have adapted so they don't have to grow an entirely new set of leaves in each short growing season –and will remain attractive long after the petunias and impatiens have faded away.

Alpine plants are adapted to porous, rocky, well–drained soil that is neutral or slightly acidic. They will not be happy in heavy clay soil. You can improve drainage by digging in sharp sand to open the soil.

In northern gardens, spring often comes and goes before it comes to stay. These "false starts" mean many northern gardeners don't grow frost-tender plants until early or mid-June.

Erratic spring temperatures are also good reason to insulate the existing plants in the garden with a thick layer of fallen leaves in autumn. These may be removed come spring (when it arrives in earnest) or left in place for strong plants to grow through. This is a excellent way to minimize weeds as well.

Stonecrop (Sedum) and hens and chicks (Sempervivum) are both extremely hardy and good looking.

Creeping thyme offers both texture and fragrance.

If low, spreading alpines such as mountain sandwort (*Arenaria montana*) or low growing hens and chicks sempervivums are planted at the bottom of a sloping rock garden or between paving stones, the effect is often referred to as an "alpine lawn." Fragrant plants are often chosen for these locations so they will release their scent when walked on—creeping or woolly thyme is a popular choice though not as hardy as many true alpines.

HARDY PERENNIALS

Hens and chicks (*Sempervivum*)	Zone 2
Golden brome grass (*Bromus inermis* 'Skinner's Gold')	Zone 1
'Prairie Traveller's Joy' Clematis (*Clematis*)	Zone 2
Bunchberry (*Cornus canadensis*)	Zone 2
Arctic campion (*Lychnis alpina*)	Zone 1
Arctic phlox (*Phlox borealis*)	Zone 2
Double sneezewort (*Achillea ptarmica* 'Ballerina')	Zone 2
Pink pussy-toes (*Antennaria dioica* 'Rubra')	Zone 3
Silver mound artemisia (*Artemisia schmidtiana* 'Nana')	Zone 2
Snow-in-summer (*Cerastium tomentosum*)	Zone 2
Lily of the valley (*Convallaria majalis*)	Zone 2
Ostrich fern (*Matteuccia struthiopteris*)	Zone 1
Wineleaf cinquefoil (*Potentilla tridentata* 'Nuuk')	Zone 2

SEASON-STRETCHING PERENNIALS

Northern gardeners shouldn't be afraid to use more perennials. There are many hardy perennials, particularly ones with interesting foliage and shapes that allow you to extend the season at both ends.

You should consider including plenty of hardy trees and shrubs in your garden designs. Native white birch (Zone 2), Siberian dogwood (Zone 2), hedge cotoneaster (Zone 3) and Saskatoon berry (Zone 2) maintain their beauty even as the seasons change, giving brilliant fall leaf colours and lovely branch structures for the winter garden.

Planting plenty of early spring bulbs among your perennials will also add greenery and colour while your perennials are just beginning to peek through the soil. I love snowdrops for this reason.

Hens and chicks (Sempervivum) require very little soil.

PLANT EARLY

If you want to get annual colour (or vegetables) sooner in your northern garden, by all means get started early. This can mean starting your vegetables and annual flowers indoors from seed or hardening them off out of doors in advance of the last frost date in your area.

Rather than wait until all risk of frost is gone, get all your hardy annuals in the ground by your average last frost date. *("Hardy annual" may sound like an oxymoron, but it refers to annuals that will take some cold and even a frost. Pansies and violas are popular, frost-hardy choices for northern gardeners.)* Half-hardy annuals and shade-loving plants can follow in the next few weeks. If you have a sudden cold snap, cover your hardy annual plants with snow, and the half-hardy ones with burlap. You may lose a few, but the extra weeks of blooms are surely well worth the risk.

Keep in mind that store-bought starter plants will need time to harden off out

Start your containers of annuals early to get a jump on spring/summer.

of doors—give them a few hours of sunshine per day, gradually increasing the time until they are completely used to a full day of outdoor exposure. Store-bought plants almost always have been delivered to the retailer directly from a greenhouse, so their growth is soft and frost-tender. (See page 75 for details on hardening off.)

Including annuals in your perennial beds and containers allows you to fill your beds with colour a few weeks early, a bonus when you're facing a too-short summer. If they do get a little frost damage to their new growth, pinch it off—you may encourage bushier growth in the long run.

Flanders Poppies.

HARDY ANNUALS

Baby's breath (*Gypsophila elegans*)
Bachelor's button (*Centaurea cyanus*)
California poppy
(*Eschscholzia californica*)
Common stock (*Matthiola incana*)
Evening primrose (*Oenothera*)
Flanders poppy
(*Papaver commutatum*)
Geraniums (*Pelargonium* x *hortorum*)
Godetia (*Godetia amoena*)
Lavatera (*Lavatera trimestris*)
Nemophila (*Nemophila*)
Nigella (*Nigella*)

Ornamental kale (*Brassica oleracea*)
Phlox (*Phlox drummondii*)
Pinks (*Dianthus chinensis*)
and (*D. caryophyllus*)
Pot marigold (*Calendula officinalis*)
Salvia (*Salvia splendens*)
Snapdragon (*Antirrhinum majus*)
Sweet alyssum (*Lobularia maritima*)
Sweet pea (*Lathyrus*)
Sweet William (*Dianthus barbatus*)
Violas and pansies (*Viola*)
Virginia stock (*Malcolmia maritima*)

Violas.

Sweet peas.

Snapdragons.

Lavatera.

A seedling thrives under a cloche.

HARDENING OFF

All early-planted annuals should be hardened off for 10 days to two weeks before planting. Hardening off prepares the young plants for their transition from the consistent growing conditions of a greenhouse or from inside of your home to the rise and fall of temperatures and moisture levels outside.

On the first day of the process, put your seedlings in a shaded spot outside for a couple of hours, and then return them indoors. With each subsequent day, leave them out for a little longer until they are used to being out of doors for the whole day. Protect them from the wind and other harsh elements. After a minimum of 10 days, they are ready to put in the ground.

A cold frame protects young plants.

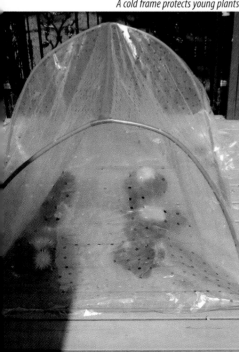

COLD FRAMES AND CLOCHES

If you like the idea of extending the growing season I recommend that you build or purchase a cold frame–a glass- or plastic-covered enclosure that acts as a miniature greenhouse.

A cold frame can be used to start and harden off plants in spring, grow late crops in fall, and overwinter marginally hardy plants. A cold frame is not difficult to make but for the non-handy person, prefabricated, collapsible cold frames are available at many garden centres, hardware stores and through mail order or online catalogues.

To protect plants planted directly in your garden from late spring frosts, use cloches and other devices like Kozy Coats (also known as the Wall O' Water), Styrofoam plant protectors, pre-cut "bandage"-style burlap, discarded plastic milk bottles (with the broad end cut out of them), portable cold frames and floating row covers at the beginning of the growing season.

By keeping the ground and the air around the plant warmer than the ambient air, these covers and enclosures encourage early growth and may very well mean the difference between enjoying a glorious garden or none at all. For more on these handy devices, check-out these web-sites:
www.mrtomato.com
www.homehardware.ca
www.leevalley.com
www.veseys.com.

WINTER PROTECTION

SNOW COVER

Snow really can be a lifesaver for perennials. The perfect winter protection, it insulates the ground, allows for air circulation and eventually provides moisture to your beds.

Deep, consistent snow cover prevents that bane of many more southerly gardeners: the freeze/thaw cycle, when rain soaks the soil, only to freeze solid the very next day and encase plant crowns in ice. And that can rot roots. When winter snow settles on my Zone 5 garden, I often shovel it off my paths and driveway to cover my more tender perennials. If you do this, be sure it doesn't contain salt, which can be deadly to all garden plants.

For the northern gardener, cooler summers and deep-freeze winters can work in your favour (this is why gardening is sometimes easier in northerly Edmonton, compared to frequently balmy Calgary). If you like a perennial that is rated as a zone higher than your

Snow cover should be encouraged, but make sure it's salt-free!

In my garden, I've found that marginally hardy plants thrive for several years and then disappear in a severe winter. It is this "game of chance" that gardeners play that makes the endeavour so interesting.

own, why not try it in a protected, southerly exposure in your garden? You may lose it over the winter, but you might also be pleasantly surprised.

If you do lose it but are passionate about the plant, consider treating it as an annual. If you're willing to take the chance that you might lose a few plants, you have more to choose from and can play with colour and texture afresh each spring.

THE CONTAINER SOLUTION

Container gardening offers a host of opportunities for the northern gardener. If you have your heart set on a perennial that you know isn't hardy for you, you can plant it in a container that can be brought into a protected space for the winter. While a plant is dormant, it doesn't need sun so it can winter over in the cold recesses of your basement.

KEY ELEMENT

OVERWINTERING

One of my best-kept secrets: the space along the inside wall of a garage where it is connected to the house is an excellent spot to overwinter marginally hardy plants. See Chapter 14 for more on container gardening.

Perennials in containers extend the possibilities.

A small conifer wrapped in Vexar mesh.

A burlap wrap will help to prevent snow damage.

EVERGREENS

Many evergreens benefit from protection during long, harsh winters. Sunny and windy winter days can dry out their needles, while snow and ice accumulation can break their branches, so it's well worth a little extra time and effort to take preventive measures in fall.

Wrap two layers of burlap around evergreens, leaving the top and bottom open about 30 centimetres (12 inches) to allow air circulation.

I have often seen home landscapes using a small screen of posts and burlap stretched around the plant. This is especially good for small or recently transplanted evergreens.

To stop the sheer weight of snow from breaking evergreen branches, a "bandage" burlap wrap can help. For sturdier protection, many northern gardeners build plywood enclosures around tender evergreens and shrubs.

ROSES

In late autumn, after ground frost and before the ground freezes thoroughly, mound soil to a depth of 30 to 40 centimetres (12 to 16 inches) around the base of each rose plant. For most parts of northern Canada, this should be done between the middle and end of October. If necessary, bring soil from another part of the garden or use triple mix (compost, topsoil and peat moss) for the task. Plants can also be covered with styrofoam rose cones for added protection. Make sure you give your roses a thorough watering to prepare them for winter.

Sure, cold zone gardening presents many challenges for Canadian gardeners, but it also brings them together. Perhaps this is why Calgary (Zone 3) has one of the biggest hort societies in the country (http://calhort.org).

KEY ELEMENT

WINTER WRAPS

Wind strong twine or cord in a spiral around small upright evergreens, or wrap them with a stretchy nylon mesh called Vexar (available at most garden centres and hardware stores) to prevent the branches from being bent down by snow and ice. This is particularly important if they are foundation plantings, which are vulnerable to ice and snow falling off the roof.

A styrofoam rose cone in place.

PART TWO
The Edible Garden

Since Mary and I moved to the country a few years ago, I have developed a vegetable garden that is about one acre in size. I view it not just as a place to produce fresh food but also as a wonderful diversion from such things as phone calls, e-mails and the details of trying to make a living.

Here, I enjoy organizing my menu for the year in rows, spacing each transplant or seed as required to produce a crop that is as near perfection as Mother Nature allows (which all too often is not all that "near"). Each day–from the sowing of the first peas in early April to the harvest of our last leek the week before the snow flies–I enjoy the challenges of keeping the pending weeds, pests and diseases at bay, while staking, pruning, deadheading and, yes, harvesting before the whole thing turns into the kind of chaos that prevents my home-grown food from ever making it to the table.

All the while, of course, I am growing our food garden organically. It is this, above all, that gives me the greatest satisfaction. In this age of "locovores"– eating food that is sourced from farms within short distances–it seems to me that the surest way to a healthy diet is to maintain control over the "inputs" as farmers like to say, including the stuff that you put in the soil and on the plants.

Growing your own fruits and vegetables is making more sense than ever.

A well-planned veggie garden.

(Left) Delicious offerings at Toronto's St. Lawrence Market.

My "Monet-inspired" apple fence.

CHAPTER NINE
Fruits

Growing your own fruit can be a very rewarding experience, and it's a wonderful activity to share with children. What better way to teach your family where their favourite foods come from? A dwarf apple tree fits into almost any Canadian garden and will produce fruit with a minimum of six hours of sunshine. Wherever you live, as long as you have adequate sun, there are fruits that will grow in your own backyard, from dwarf trees

'Boyne' is an ultra-hardy, summer-bearing raspberry.

to a few raspberries in containers. (Choose a large container at least 80 centimetres [32 inches] in diameter or about the size of a half barrel or bushel basket and use a soil-based sandy mixture that drains well.) The key to a successful harvest is to choose fruits and berries best suited to your growing conditions.

Many fruits are well suited to container growing—particularly raspberries, strawberries, blueberries, dwarf peaches and dwarf apples. Just keep your growing zone in mind as you make your selection.

RASPBERRIES

(*Rubus idaeus*)

Raspberries are known as "bramble fruits' because they have thorns to protect their crop. Bramble fruit are perennials and the canes they send out bear fruit in their second year. A healthy raspberry patch will bear a productive crop of fruit for up to six or

seven years before needing to be replanted. Raspberries grow best in warm summers where there is plenty of moisture. They prefer established beds to reduce the threat of cutworm. There are *summer-bearing* raspberries, which have a big flush of fruit and then they're done, and *ever-bearing* (sometimes called fall-bearing) ones, which fruit a bit later but keep producing berries until frost.

I mulch my raspberries with a 10-centimetre (four-inch) thick layer of finely ground-up pine or cedar bark mulch. This retains moisture, reducing watering by about 70 percent and makes weeding almost a non-event. A 30-centimetre (12-inch) layer of clean straw can also substitute for bark mulch.

SOIL REQUIREMENTS

Raspberries like rich, fertile, well-drained soil on the acidic side (with a pH of 6.0). Triple mix (one-third sand,

one-third peat moss and one-third topsoil) is best. One-year-old rooted canes should be planted so the soil level is two centimetres above the root union on the canes. Dig in bone meal and plenty of well-rotted manure or compost before planting. Add water to the hole as you fill with triple mix. Mulch the soil with 10 centimetres (four inches) of bark mulch, and water in dry weather.

LIGHT REQUIREMENTS

Although raspberries will tolerate a little shade, they are happier and yield more fruit in full sun.

SPACING

Raspberries can be planted in spring or fall. Keep 45 centimetres (18 inches) of space between plants and at least two metres (six feet) between rows. The farther apart you plant the rows the better the air circulation, which reduces the chance of disease.

RASPBERRY SUPPORT

Canes are usually firm enough that they can support each other when planted in rows. A trellis system can be used to make it easier to harvest the fruit. Drive a wooden post into the ground at the end of each row and run a wire along either side of the row as a support.

PRUNING

After planting, trim the canes to nine inches high. In the first growing season, remove flowers to allow the plants to conserve energy. In the second year, you will enjoy your first crop, though not a very plentiful one; be patient as the best is yet to come!

In early spring, remove any winter-killed canes at ground level.

Summer-fruiting varieties produce fruit on the previous year's growth. Right after the last berries have been picked, cut out the canes that have fruited so new canes can take their place. Prune out any suckers growing between established plants.

Ever-bearing varieties produce fruit on canes in their first season. Cut the canes down to the ground after harvest in late fall.

PESTS AND DISEASES

Botrytis cane wilt causes new canes to wilt. Verticillium wilt results in canes wilting suddenly in hot, dry weather. Anthracnose, also known as cane spot, produces purple spots on the leaves and grey growth on the stems. The best way to deal with any of these is to cut out the infected stems as they appear and throw them out. Do not put them in your composter. If the problem persists, I spray with garden sulfur first and, if it persists on new growth, I apply Bordo spray, which contains copper, a deterrent to many plant diseases.

Powdery mildew can cover the foliage with a white powder. This is a problem most prevalent in heavy soils and during wet seasons. To discourage it, I thin my crop allowing five to eight centimetres (two to three inches) between mature canes.

Aphids can be sprayed off with a hose or treated with insecticidal soap.

Raspberry fruitworm shows up as dried-up patches near the stalk of berries, caused by the beetle larvae as

RASPBERRY VARIETIES & HARDINESS

VARIETY	HARDINESS ZONE	DESCRIPTION
'Boyne'	2	Ultra-hardy and very reliable. Dark red, medium-sized berries. Summer-bearing. Recommended for Prairies.
'Nova'	3	Almost thornless. Bright red, medium-sized berry. Summer-bearing.
'Fall Gold'	4	Sweet yellow berries. Ever-bearing variety.
'Kiwi Gold'	4	Most popular yellow variety. Mid-season harvest.
'Perron's Red'	4	Ever-bearing variety. Large, conical red berries. Harvest from last week of July until frost.
'Sweet Treat'	3	Ever-bearing variety. Abundant production in the first year.
'Autumn Bliss'	3	An early ever-bearing variety, fruiting in late August. Cold hardy and tolerates high temperatures.
'Cumberland'	5	Reliable and vigorous growth. Plentiful shiny black berries. Self-pollinates.
'Heritage'	3	Ever-bearing variety with firm fruit. Very productive. Recommended for Prairies.

they feed on the buds and the berries. Treat fruitworm with organic rotenone powder when beetle larvae are evident.

WEEDING AND FEEDING

Raspberry plants have shallow roots that can be easily disturbed. Take care when removing weeds to avoid damaging the root system of your crop.

A successful raspberry crop is hungry: I recommend feeding once each month in April, May and June with an organic fertilizer like blood and bone meal. Alternatively, rake back the mulch and place three centimetres (1 1/2 inches) of composted cattle, steer or horse manure at the root zone each spring, then rake the mulch back into place.

Fresh picked raspberries.

STRAWBERRIES
(*Fragaria* hybrids)

Strawberry plants are hardy perennials (some to Zone 2) and tend to grow aggressively with very little help. Their public enemy #1 is weeds. Because strawberry plants are low-growing, they can become choked out with tall weeds very quickly. For the first two years, hand-weeding is in order. Planting in well-prepared soil that is as weed-free as possible in the first place will save you many hours of maintenance.

The original plant, also called the mother plant, will send out runners. These stems put down roots and form daughter (son?) plants. It takes only three or four years for a strawberry patch to become overgrown, which results in less fruiting. Proper maintenance is essential in prolonging the life of your strawberry plants. Of course, you could choose to grow strawberries as annual plants. The

ever-bearing varieties are an excellent choice for containers as they will produce fruit throughout the season.

TYPES OF STRAWBERRIES

Summer-fruiting strawberries, also known as June-bearing, bear fruit over two to three weeks in the summer.

Ever-bearing strawberries have their first crop in the summer and a second crop in autumn.

'Veestar' strawberries.

Day-neutral strawberries bear fruit throughout the summer, except during very hot weather.

Alpine strawberries have a long fruiting season and bear small fruits. Often grown as an ornamental for the edge of flower gardens, these strawberries do not send out runners and require less maintenance than other types.

SOIL REQUIREMENTS

Strawberries like rich, fertile soil that is slightly alkaline with a pH of 5.5 to 6.5. Good drainage (i.e., a sandy soil) ensures plants will not rot and helps to avoid disease problems. Double-dig* strawberry beds in the fall, adding plenty of compost or composted manure. Strawberries should be planted in early spring but they can successfully be started in the fall. Holes for plants should be wide enough to allow for root growth. Place plants in holes so that the crowns are just below the soil surface. Water new plantings well and mulch with 15 to 20 centimetres (six to eight inches) of straw. The plants will need consistent watering once the fruits form.

LIGHT REQUIREMENTS

Strawberries need a warm, sunny site; a south-facing slope is ideal. A spot with full sun allows later fruits on the ever-bearing types to ripen.

SPACING

Grow strawberries in slightly raised rows. Rows should be 75 centimetres (30 inches) apart to allow for easy harvest. Plant summer-fruiting varieties 50 centimetres (20 inches) apart and ever-bearing types 20 centimetres (eight inches) apart. Summer-bearing strawberries are spaced farther apart to allow room for runners to grow. These should be removed in the first year and placed in another bed to mature.

Straw is an ideal mulch for strawberries.

KEY ELEMENT

*DOUBLE-DIGGING
A method of deep cultivation that involves systematically digging a bed and loosening the soil to the depth of two shovel blades.

STRAWBERRY VARIETIES & HARDINESS

VARIETY	HARDINESS ZONE	FEATURES
'Veestar'	2	Early summer-fruiting. High yields of dark red, medium - sized berries. Recommended for Prairies.
'Kent'	2	Mid-season summer-fruiting. High yields of bright red fruit. Recommended for Prairies.
'Cavendish'	2	Mid-season summer-fruiting. Can be harvested over an extended period of time. Recommended for Prairies.
'Tristar'	4	Day-neutral. Produces through summer and fall.
'Ozark Beauty'	4	Ever-bearing. Performs well in pots or the garden. Excellent disease resistance.
'Quinalt'	4	Ever-bearing. Self-pollinating. Resistant to leaf scorch, leaf spot and root rot.
'Delmarvel'	4	Summer-fruiting. Excellent disease resistance.
'Earliglow'	5	Summer-fruiting. Resistant to leaf scorch and verticillium wilt.

Strawberry runner looking to put down roots.

SUPPORT

If it is manageable, lift the berries off the ground and place them on the straw mulch to keep them clean by preventing contact with the soil, improve air circulation and protect the berries from ground-dwelling insects.

PRUNING

In the first year, pinch off runners close to the parent plant or the plant will waste energy on new plant production rather than fruit production. Also in the first year, remove all initial flowers from all varieties. Ever-bearing strawberries will produce a second set of blossoms and then a light, midsummer crop. Fruit production will be strongest every second year. I recommend that you plant a second crop a year after the first, to have a robust harvest every year.

In late fall, cut back strawberry tops to about seven centimetres (three inches) by raising your lawn mower to its highest setting and mowing the existing crop down. Cover with an organic winter mulch like clean straw, about 10 centimetres (four inches) deep.

PESTS AND DISEASES

One piece of advice that is indispensable where strawberries are concerned: purchase clean, disease-resistant plants in the first place. In other words, buy from a reliable and preferably local source.

If you see diseased plants, immediately remove them and burn them. Watch also for a wide variety of insects that enjoy munching on your strawberry crop, especially when the fruit is just about ripe for the picking!

Keep leaves and fruit off the soil with straw mulch to help deter pests. Protect the fruit from birds with bird-netting, a floating row cover, or aluminum plates or old CDs suspended over plants. The noise and the light reflections will deter a host of pests.

Finally, practice a good farming technique by rotating your crop. Strawberries are a member of the Solanaceae family; therefore, do not plant strawberries where other members of the same family (tomatoes, peppers, potatoes and eggplants) have been grown.

BLUEBERRIES
(*Vaccinium*)

Hybrid blueberries are hardy to Zone 6; native varieties to Zone 3.

When it comes to eating for better health, the lowly blueberry is getting top billing from nutritionists due to its high antioxidant content. It is considered to be one of the most valuable whole foods that you can eat. Luckily for us Canadians, there is a bounty of wild blueberries throughout much of the country—Oxford, N.S., is the "Wild Blueberry Capital" of Canada—and we have lots of agricultural land that seems perfectly suited to growing them under cultivation—British Columbia leads the way there.

'Bluecrop' blueberries.

SPACING
Most blueberries are self-fertile but for better crops and bigger berries, choose two or more varieties and alternate them as you plant the row so they will cross-pollinate. For even better pollination, plant three—one of one variety and two of another. Space the plants 90 centimetres to 1.5 metres (three to five feet) apart. Some varieties need more space—check the information on the plant tags. The rows should be two to 2.4 metres (six to eight feet) apart.

Blueberry shrubs are deciduous and produce berries in late summer. The fruits turn from green to red to blue as they ripen. The plants are productive for many years and do not require a lot of care. Many gardeners choose to grow highbush blueberry shrubs (*Vaccinium corymbosum*) for their ornamental qualities—they have beautiful white flowers in spring and striking orange-red foliage in fall.

SOIL REQUIREMENTS
Blueberries like richly organic, well-drained, acidic soil, with a pH between 4 and 5. Ideally, the soil should be moist with plenty of peat. The plants should be fertilized each spring with well-rotted manure at least four centimetres (1 1/2 inches) deep and mulched with a layer at least six centimetres (2 1/2 inches) thick of evergreen needles like spruce or pine.

Blueberries are most often planted in the early spring in cool climates (the exception, of course, is on the Pacific coast of British Columbia).

Dig holes wide enough to accommodate the plant roots. Add water to the hole and let it drain before placing the plant in it. Set the plant so the existing soil line on the plant is level with the soil surface. Fill the hole with soil, mounding it around the plant and mulch the root zone with pine or spruce needles. Water well.

LIGHT REQUIREMENTS
Although blueberries will tolerate partial shade, they need sun for the fruit to ripen, and crop most vigorously in full sun.

KEY ELEMENT

ACIDIFY THE SOIL
In areas where alkaline soil predominates like Southern Ontario and Quebec, it is very helpful to acidify the soil twice a year by applying powdered sulfur. I use about 200 grams (seven ounces) per plant, once in spring and again in late summer or early fall. I much prefer this method to using aluminum sulfate, which is known to persist in the soil for long periods of time.

BLUEBERRY VARIETIES & HARDINESS

VARIETY	HARDINESS ZONE	FEATURES
'Chippewa'	4	Mid-season variety. Sweet, medium-sized, light-blue berries.
'Blueray'	4	Mid-season variety. Tight clusters of large, dark-blue berries.
'Bluecrop'	4	Mid-season variety. Loose clusters of large, light-blue berries.
'Bluetta'	3	Early crop. Large, firm berries. Recommended for Prairies.
'Patriot'	3	Early to mid-season crop. Prefers heavier soils. Cold-hardy and compact in size. Recommended for Prairies.
'Spartan'	5	Extra large berries. Requires well-drained sandy loam.
'Rubel'	4	Excellent for baking. Mid-season. Self-fertile.
'Sunshine Blue'	6	Small dark-blue berries. Ornamental flowers and fall colour.

PRUNING

I recommend that you remove flowers in the first year to allow the plant to conserve energy. In the next two years, prune only dead or damaged branches. From the fourth year on, remove up to four of the oldest shoots (but no more than one-third of the plant) to encourage new growth, open up the branching, and increase air circulation. Pruning allows you to keep plants at a reasonable size for harvesting the crop, and lets light into the bush to ripen the fruit. If plants grow too large or dense, they can be pruned during the winter months but generally the best time for pruning is within a few weeks of the finished harvest.

PESTS AND DISEASES

Birds and rabbits love blueberries, so you may need to cover the bushes with

Fresh picked—ready to eat!

netting to protect your precious harvest. Blueberries do not have any serious pests or diseases. Most modern cultivars are bred for disease resistance.

BUSH FRUITS

CURRANTS
(*Ribes*)

Hardy to Zone 3 and one of the oldest fruit-bearing bushes used in Canadian gardens, currants were grown by pioneer settlers in many parts of the country.

Growing up to 90 centimetres (three feet) high and wide, the bushes make ornamental hedges as well as a practical food source. Once established, they are hardy, low-maintenance and are considered one of the few berry bushes that will grow and bear fruit reliably in partial shade. During dry weather, it is necessary to supply water as the fruit develops. Mulching is very helpful. Do not water as the fruit ripens or the skins will split.

LIGHT REQUIREMENTS

The fruit needs the sun to ripen, though not necessarily a whole day of sun. West exposure is best, where the sun is strongest and the breeze generally more

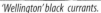

'Wellington' black currants.

reliable. Currants are susceptible to mildew so the better the air circulation, the better your currants. Annual pruning allows light to penetrate the plant and reach the fruit.

SPACING

Space bushes 1.2 metres (four feet) apart.

Continued on page 89.

WHAT WE CAN LEARN FROM FARMERS

"It has taken me 50 years, but finally I have a home in the country…and I now bump into farmers every time I pump gas at the local station. I chat it up with farmers over a burger at Sam's Restaurant about two kilometres down the road. I even have a brother-in-law next door who proudly calls himself a full-time farmer.

It's handy, having this rich resource so close. Whenever I need advice about the land, I know where to go. And when I come back home, I usually have a dozen cobs of corn in the car as proof of where I have been.

In this first year of living in my new four-hectare (10-acre) garden, I have learned that farmers and gardeners have a whole lot in common, especially where stewardship of the land is concerned.

For example, I wanted to sow some clover this fall as a "green manure" to enhance the soil quality in my veggie garden. I tilled the earth in October and was all set to sow the clover seed when I thought better of it. I would talk to my neighbour Guy just to be sure. "The best time to sow clover is in the first two weeks of April," said Guy. "You just spread the seed on the surface of the soil and the last few frosts of spring will drive the seed down for you. Then we will get lots of spring rain. No need to rake it or cultivate. Just let nature do her work."

It's that easy? I said to myself. I let on to Guy that I knew this all along and just needed confirmation.

Dan Needles, author of the great Canadian *Wingfield Farm* series, tells the story of a farmer who was talking with a new neighbour who had escaped the city for the country life.

"Why are there so many rocks on the farms around here?" asked the newbie farmer.

"They're there to knock the soil off your implements as you plow the fields," replied the farmer.

"And why is that guy over there piling his up like that?" asked the inquisitive city boy, pointing across the concession road.

Said the farmer, "Oh, that. Well, he just took delivery of those and he'll be spreading them any time now."

As I have learned, farmers on average have an above-average sense of humour. And they don't take themselves so seriously that they can't laugh at themselves, or each other. And while farmers may have fun with city folk—and vice versa—they have much to teach.

To grow a healthy crop of anything and to grow it well takes time, experience, planning, no end of patience and lots of hard work. Not to mention a large measure of faith that the rains will come—and go—and the sun will shine on a timely basis.

Try to farm or garden without a large measure of faith and you are in for frustrating days. Bring together the soil, water, sun and a packet of seeds and you have a risk that is worth taking. I think gardeners and farmers should get along very well, like fishermen and hunters do. Hikers and campers. You get the idea.

The farmers I know have generally come from farming families. Many have made a living on the same land for generations. None of them look at their work as a short-term job, a rung in the ladder to somewhere greater. They have arrived and the land is their best friend.

It only makes sense, then, that farmers respect soil and water for the future income they represent. Modern farming practices call for less disruption of the soil than years ago, a reduction in the use of chemicals and a long-term view to soil quality and productivity.

As a gardener, I plan on picking their brains for a long time yet."

Mark

(Excerpt from A Sandbox of a Different Kind by Mark Cullen)

'Primus' white currants.

SOIL REQUIREMENTS FOR CURRANTS

Currant bushes like cool, moist soil. If you have sandy loam, mulch the root zone with a four-centimetre (1 1/2-inch) layer of well-rotted manure each spring to help retain moisture.

BUSH FRUITS

CURRANTS

PRUNING

Plant in either spring or fall. Prune a two-year-old shrub to 15 centimetres (six inches) above ground level the first season. After that, do not prune for four years until the bush is established. In the fifth season, prune after fruiting or in fall or winter. Cut back the tips of all main branches by trimming just above a bud, and remove the oldest wood from the shrub. Leave only six healthy canes on each bush. Currants are very forgiving plants and respond to pruning by sending out new growth and ample fruit.

PESTS AND DISEASES

Currants can be host to white pine blister rust, a fungal disease that doesn't bother the currants but can be deadly to pines. Ontario's Ministry of Agriculture recommends planting currants (and gooseberries) no closer than 300 metres (1,000 feet) to white pines.

Watch for caterpillars and mildew on leaves. To treat powdery mildew, apply garden sulfur after the blooms have set fruit.

The biggest threat to a currant crop is the birds. Cover the bushes with netting to protect the fruit.

'Red Lake' red currants.

CURRANT VARIETIES & HARDINESS

VARIETY	HARDINESS ZONE	FEATURES
'Wellington'	3	Large clusters of black currants. Produces fruit in two to three years. Recommended for Prairies
'Crandall'	3	Black fruits contain five times the vitamin C of oranges. Excellent for jams, juice and syrup.
'Consort'	3	Resistant to white pine blister rust. Black fruit has a black-berry flavour. Excellent bird forage or windbreak plants.
'Red Lake'	3	High yield of small red berries. Easy to grow.
'Cherry'	3	Resistant to powdery mildew. Hardiest and best yielding red currant.
'Primus'	3	Compact bush bears up to nine kg (20 lbs) of white currants per plant.
'White Imperial'	3	Richest and sweetest flavour of all currants. Similar to red currants in size.

Gooseberries develop on thorny canes that grow 90 centimetres (three feet) high and then ramble. Plant in autumn or winter if the ground is not frozen.

GOOSEBERRIES

(*Ribes grossularia*)

A variety of gooseberries are available for the home garden. Some, like the pink-flushed 'Pixwell', are sour and wonderful for jam. Others are sweet enough for eating fresh, though less hardy than 'Pixwell'. Most gooseberries are hardy to Zone 3.

SOIL REQUIREMENTS

They like cool, moist, rich soil with plenty of loam. Gooseberries do not like hot, dry, sandy sites. An eastern or northeastern exposure is best. Mulch with a five-centimetre (two-inch) layer of well-rotted manure each spring. They need watering only when the growing season is very dry.

LIGHT REQUIREMENTS

Plant in light shade in areas with hot summers.

SPACING

Plant bushes about 1.5 metres (four to five feet) apart. After planting, prune back to four or five above-ground buds.

PRUNING

Gooseberries produce most of their fruit on two- and three-year-old wood. After the first year, prune all but four or six of the healthiest canes. Subsequently, each winter, cut out the heaviest and oldest canes 15 centimetres (six inches) above the root stock. After pruning, a healthy gooseberry bush should have nine to 12 shoots (three to four shoots each of one-, two- and three-year-old shoots). Any shoots older than three years should be cut out.

PESTS AND DISEASES

Gooseberries are vulnerable to birds, aphids, sawfly and mildew. Good air circulation and the application of garden sulfur helps to reduce mildew.

Gooseberries enjoy light shade (an eastern exposure) and quality loam.

GOOSEBERRY VARIETIES & HARDINESS

VARIETY	HARDINESS ZONE	FEATURES
'Captivator'	3	Very hardy. Good resistance to mildew. Tall and nearly spineless. Produces reddish fruit in two to three years.
'Welcome'	3	Produces large, tart, red fruit.
'Poorman'	3	Mildew resistant. Large red fruit on a compact plant.
'Langley Gage'	3	Translucent white fruit. Produces a large crop of bite-sized, sweet gooseberries.

drained, even sandy, and moderately fertile, with a relatively high pH. A range from 6.0 to 7.0 is adequate, depending on the variety chosen. Each growing season, fertilize the root zone of each grapevine with a four-centimetre (1 1/2-inch) layer of composted manure.

LIGHT REQUIREMENTS

Grapes grown in warm regions of wine country are trained along open supports of posts and wires. This allows air to circulate around the plant, and sunlight to reach the fruit. In colder regions (Zones 4 and 5), grapes require a sunny, sheltered wall. Vines are either trained along horizontal wires spaced 30 centimetres (12 inches) apart across the wall, or simply incorporated into the ornamental landscape as a useful twining vine.

SPACING

Plant grapevines in the spring, deep enough to let one bud show above soil level. Space plants at least 1.5 metres (five feet) apart, and rows 2.5 metres (eight feet) apart.

PRUNING

Pruning grapes requires regular attention and can be a lot of fun. The idea is to provide a strong root system and sturdy trunk. There are many methods to choose from.

Summer pruning focuses on controlling the amount of foliage so the plant's energy will be concentrated on fruit production. Side branches which do not have fruit are pruned back to five or six leaves. The side branches with fruit are pruned back to two leaves beyond the last bunch of grapes.

Winter pruning is performed mid-winter. All side branches which have produced fruit are pruned back to the

GRAPES

(Vitis vinifera)

In my Zone 5 garden I grow grapes for the "fun of it," enjoying the cover that the vines produce reliably every year and, in good years, a tasty harvest. Grapes require a long, hot summer and prefer a mild winter. For the most part, they perform best in a Zone 6 garden, though the old Concord and Niagara grapes will produce in Zone 5 quite reliably and even in Zone 3 or 4 when planted in a microclimate that is protected from the north and west winds in winter.

SOIL REQUIREMENTS

The soil for grapes needs to be well

strongest bud from the main leader. Allow side branches to grow out each year and tie them to the support wires.

PESTS AND DISEASES

Watch for downy mildew, anthracnose and black rot (a fungus which shrivels the fruits, turning them hard and black). These can be treated with garden sulfur for mild problems and Bordo mixture for more severe ones. Bird netting is essential to keep birds off the grapes.

'Concord' grapes, a thing of beauty.

'Niagara' white grapes growing on a telephone pole on Toronto Island.

GRAPE VARIETIES & HARDINESS

VARIETY	HARDINESS ZONE	FEATURES
'Kay Gray'	3	White grape. Medium-sized fruit suitable for wine or as table grapes.
'Niagara'	4	Excellent choice for wine production. Used commercially for white grape juice. Green table grapes with lots of flavour.
'Concord'	5	A very popular variety. Produces large bunches of sweet, flavourful fruit.
'Valiant'	3	Sweet, dark-purple grape. Very hardy and productive. Ripens in late August.
'Agawam'	5	Red-purple grapes. Suitable for wine and as a table grape.
'Canadice'	4	Red seedless variety. Large compact bunches. Harvest mid-September.
'Himrod'	5	High-quality white grape. Perfectly round and seedless fruit. Ripens late September.
'Vandal Cliche'	3	White grapes ideal for wine or as table grapes. Very hardy and productive. Harvest mid-September.
'St-Croix'	4	Sweet blue grape. Very productive. Harvest at beginning of September.

TREE FRUITS

APPLES

(*Malus domestica*)

A mature apple tree is more than a source of homegrown fruit; it is also a beautiful specimen in the landscape. Showy flowers lead to a summer harvest when trees are well-maintained and planted in the correct conditions. Espaliered apple trees produce large crops and add beauty to the garden. Most apples are hardy to Zone 4. Plant two or more varieties that bloom at the same time to ensure pollination. The pollen of some apple varieties is sterile ('Jonagold', 'Mutsu' and 'Winesap', for example) so they are not a good choice as pollenizers.

SOIL REQUIREMENTS

The soil should be a rich, moist, well-drained loam. Apple trees will withstand a variety of soil conditions as long as the location is not waterlogged.

LIGHT REQUIREMENTS

Apple trees prefer full sun but will tolerate some shade.

PRUNING

Thin out the fruit crop in summer to improve the size and quality of the remaining apples. Prune trees in late winter before new growth begins. Remove all dead, diseased and crossing branches, and any vertical suckers. The goal of pruning is to open up the structure of the tree to improve air circulation and light penetration.

'Cortland' apples are one of my favourites.

PESTS AND DISEASES

Apples are susceptible to codling moth, apple maggot, cedar-apple rust and fire blight, among other common insects and diseases.

Spray apple trees with dormant oil and lime sulfur to control a wide range of over-wintering insects and diseases. Many problems can be controlled by maintaining a healthy, vigorous tree. Water deeply and maintain a thick layer of mulch around the root zone. Proper pruning for air circulation helps reduce mildew problems.

My 'Liberty' apples, grown organically of course.

APPLE VARIETIES & HARDINESS

VARIETY	HARDINESS ZONE	FEATURES
'McIntosh'	4	Tender red skin with crisp white flesh. Blooms early. Requires a pollenizer.
'Red Delicious'	5	Mid-October dessert apple. Requires a pollenizer.
'Cortland'	4	Extremely cold hardy. Pure white flesh with tangy flavour. Harvest end of September.
'Empire'	4b	A cross between 'Red Delicious' and 'McIntosh'. Harvest in October.
'Golden Delicious'	5	Conical yellow fruit. Trees are quite productive. Good choice for pies.

My 'Bosc' pears. Note hail damage on lower right fruit. It's cosmetic only; the fruit tastes fine.

PRUNING

Pear trees do not generally lend themselves to regular pruning. In fact, heavy pruning can make the tree susceptible to fire blight.

However, come spring you should remove dead, damaged or crossing branches. Cut back the main trunk and upper branches to a manageable height. Remove vertical suckers. Thin branches from the interior of the crown to increase sunlight and air penetration and keep the tree healthy and attractive.

PEARS

(*Pyrus communis*)

Pear trees grown on their own roots become very large trees that can be difficult to prune, spray and harvest. Also, the fruit is damaged when it falls from high branches. For these reasons, pears are grown on quince root stocks producing smaller and more compact trees. Don't plant pear trees too deeply as this can bury the graft union and cause future problems. Most pear varieties are hardy to Zone 5.

Pears require good air circulation and a site that is slightly elevated or sloping. This protects early blooms from frost damage, which can occur in low-lying areas or frost pockets. Pears need a second variety planted within 13 metres (40 feet) for cross-pollination.

SOIL REQUIREMENTS

The soil must be rich, well-drained yet moist with a good loamy texture.

LIGHT REQUIREMENTS

Pear trees require full sun.

PESTS AND DISEASES

Pears suffer fewer problems than apple trees. Fire blight is a common problem, producing symptoms similar to scorch. Prune and dispose of damaged parts as soon as they appear.

'Bartlett' pear. I love pear trees' clean, glossy foliage.

Here's a pear that thinks it's a Picasso painting.

PEAR VARIETIES & HARDINESS

VARIETY	HARDINESS ZONE	FEATURES
'Bartlett'	5	Excellent for fresh eating and canning. Fruit is green when picked, yellow when ripe. Susceptible to fire blight.
'Anjou'	4	Fruit is large and stays green when ripe. Fairly resistant to fire blight.
'Bosc'	5	Fine-flavoured dessert pear. Fruit has russetted skin. Excellent pollenizer. Hardy tree but susceptible to fire blight.

'Mount Royal' plum tree.

PLUMS
(*Prunus domestica*)

Plums are popular in the home garden because they don't require a great deal of space. Most varieties will produce crops from their fifth year. Plum blossoms are susceptible to late frost damage. Plant plum trees in a slightly raised or sloping location with good air circulation. Cold can damage blossoms in low-lying areas and frost pockets.

SOIL REQUIREMENTS

Plums need a well-drained soil with plenty of organic matter to hold moisture. Do not plant plums in alkaline soil—they will not prosper.

LIGHT REQUIREMENTS

Plum trees need as much sun as they can get, so full sun all the way.

PRUNING

Plums are often grown as standards because the branches are heavy-fruiting and pull the branches downward. Remove dead and diseased wood in late winter.

PESTS AND DISEASES

Plums are relatively pest free. Brown rot, which causes spots on the fruit, can be a problem in some years. These spots lead to grey mold. Pick up and destroy dropped fruit to control this disease. Aphids, mites and leafrollers can be treated with insecticidal soap sprays.

Growing your own fruit trees and berry bushes is one of the most satisfying things that you can do in a Canadian garden, if you ask me! And the beauty of it is that you don't need a vast amount of space to do it.

Japanese plums.

PLUM VARIETIES & HARDINESS

VARIETY	HARDINESS ZONE	FEATURES
'Mount Royal'	4	European plum. Medium-sized fruit with blue skin and yellow flesh. Self-pollinating.
'Patterson Pride'	2b	A Japanese hybrid. Very hardy dwarf tree with a weeping form.
'Pembina'	3	Prairie-hardy. Large thick-skinned fruit is reddish-blue with yellow flesh. Requires a pollinator.
'Fiebing'	3b	Exceptionally hardy Prairie plum. Dark skin and yellow flesh. Self-pollinating but another plum nearby will increase fruit yield.

A perfect mid-June evening in our veggie garden. Spiral stakes have just been set for the season.

CHAPTER TEN
Vegetables

My vegetable garden is my sandbox. This is where I go to enjoy the rhythm and stroke of hoeing weeds, the careful pinching and twining of tomatoes on a spiral stake and, ultimately, the satisfaction of growing my own food: fresh to the table and preserved in the freezer for off-season consumption.

Your vegetable garden provides the very best opportunity to enjoy the benefits of organic gardening. After all, this is the stuff that you are going to take from the garden and put in your mouth—and your family's mouths—and it should be the healthiest and safest food around.

It is in your power to provide this quality of food right from your own garden: I consider that notion alone pretty exciting.

The best advice I can give to someone planning their first vegetable garden is "start small." Even a modest planting can produce more servings than one family can possibly consume. If you try to plant a few vegetables the first year, you can increase your plantings the following year based on your consumption and growing success.

As I have said before in this book, *your ultimate success will hinge on proper soil preparation.* This is truer of vegetables than any other form of gardening. The results of your "ground work" will make it all the way to your mouth—and what could be a better judge?

The second most important piece of advice that I can give is to locate your veggie garden in as much sun as possible. Except for leaf lettuce and spinach, your vegetables will require as much sun as you can give them.

Tall tomato spirals are a terrific labour-saving device: there's no tying and they last forever. Staking your tomatoes like this will double your crop.

A well-planned, prepared and maintained urban veggie garden.

Vegetables like soil that is loose and friable (meaning easy to turn over and dig), enabling roots to grow readily and quickly. This is particularly true of root vegetables such as carrots, parsnips, radishes and potatoes. Their roots will often fork or become misshapen in compacted or heavy soil. Only a few, like broccoli and rutabaga, will manage in clay-based soils.

SOIL PREP 101

Soil, as always, is paramount. Most vegetables need a slightly acidic soil with a pH of approximately 6.5. Many vegetables are heavy feeders, so the soil has to be nutrient-rich from the outset with plenty of organic matter. Before planting, the entire vegetable garden should be covered with at least three centimetres (a generous inch) of finished compost. You can turn this layer of compost under with a rototiller or spade if you like, or let the earthworms do it for you. They will take a few months to do the job, but that is fine.

If you have inherited poor soil, you don't have to give up on vegetables. You can create a raised bed by mounding triple mix 30 to 40 centimetres (12 to 16 inches) higher than grade to achieve good fertility and excellent drainage. You can also use raised boxes and containers filled with a quality triple mix (equal proportions of peat, compost and topsoil).

LIGHT

Most vegetables and herbs need no fewer than six hours of sunlight a day. If possible, plant your vegetables in a south-facing location. If that isn't available, choose a southeast or southwest exposure.

Where exposure to sunshine is a problem, you can increase the reflected light on your vegetables by using light-coloured mulches and even aluminum foil on the surface of the soil. You will be surprised at how effective this can be in an east- or northeast-facing vegetable garden.

If you have room enough to plant your vegetables in rows, orient them north and south, and plant the tallest vegetables at the east end with plant heights decreasing toward the west end. This way, the tall plants will not shade the shorter plants later in the day as the sun moves from east to west.

Tall plants include staked or twining vegetables such as pole beans, peas on a trellis, staked tomatoes, corn or asparagus. Mid-sized plants include bush beans, potatoes and broccoli; lettuce, carrots and onions are usually the shortest vegetables.

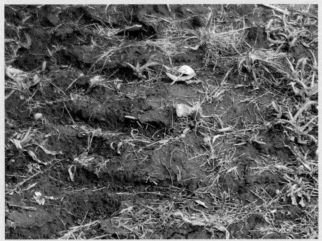

1. Choose a sunny spot.

2. Amend the soil and rototill or dig over by hand.

3. Using a guide string, dig a trench 8-10 cm (3-4 inches) deep.

4. Cut potatoes into 3-4 cm (1-1/2 inch) pieces and place in trench.

5. Firm the soil over them and water well.

6. Mound the soil up around the growing plants.

A mulch between rows keeps your garden tidy, minimizes weeds and retains moisture.

WATER AND MULCH

Vegetables need daily watering when at the seedling stage, with consistent watering as the surface of the soil dries thereafter. Be wary of trees in any area you want to plant vegetables. Not only do they create shade but they also deplete the soil of moisture and nutrients. If possible, plant vegetables beyond the drip line of mature trees.

In exposed locations, more watering may be needed due to the drying effects of the wind. You can overcome this by planting a row of sunflowers on the west and north side of the garden as a temporary summer "wall," and also by putting down a thick layer of organic mulch.

This not only helps to retain moisture but also encourages earthworm activity and fosters microbial activity in the soil. I recommend a mulch of finely ground-up pine or cedar bark but a layer of straw at least 15 centimetres (six inches) deep or even 12 to 15 pages of newspaper work quite well, too. The mulch will also reduce your weeding dramatically, saving you countless hours and giving you the opportunity to do the really important stuff—such as harvest fresh produce as it becomes ripe.

PLANTING TIMES

The best planting times for individual vegetables are often given in the number of weeks before or after the last spring frost. Likewise, the sowing of late–harvest vegetables is usually indicated by the number of weeks before the first fall frost. You will have to know what the average last frost and first frost dates are for your area before you plant. Your local weather bureau should be able to provide average dates for you, but turn over the page for a chart with the the dates for major Canadian cities. Go to www.weatheroffice.gc.ca for more information.

A fresh cabbage cut at Farintosh farms.

Canadian designed and manufactured, this "heart breaker" sprinkler saves water.

FIRST AND LAST FROST DATES FOR CANADIAN CITIES

CITY	PROV	GROWING SEASON (LENGTH IN DAYS)	LAST SPRING FROST	FIRST FALL FROST	CITY	PROV	GROWING SEASON (LENGTH IN DAYS)	LAST SPRING FROST	FIRST FALL FROST
Athabasca	AB	88	Jun. 1	Aug. 29	Aklavik	NT	76	Jun. 13	Aug. 31
Calgary	AB	114	May 23	Sept. 15	Fort Simpson	NT	81	Jun. 3	Aug. 24
Edmonton	AB	138	May 7	Sept. 23	Yellowknife	NT	110	May 27	Sept. 15
Grande Prairie	AB	117	May 18	Sept. 13	Barrie	ON	112	May 26	Sept. 16
Lethbridge	AB	123	May 17	Sept. 18	Hamilton	ON	168	Apr. 29	Oct. 15
Medicine Hat	AB	128	May 16	Sept. 22	Kapuskasing	ON	87	Jun. 12	Sept. 8
Peace River	AB	99	May 26	Sept. 3	Kingston	ON	160	May 2	Oct. 10
Red Deer	AB	106	May 25	Sept. 9	Kitchener	ON	139	May 11	Sept. 29
Abbotsford	BC	177	Apr. 24	Oct. 18	London	ON	151	May 9	Oct. 8
Chilliwack	BC	216	Apr. 6	Nov. 9	Ottawa	ON	151	May 6	Oct. 5
Dawson Creek	BC	84	Jun. 5	Aug. 29	Owen Sound	ON	155	May 12	Oct. 15
Kamloops	BC	156	Jun. 1	Oct. 5	Peterborough	ON	124	May 18	Sept. 20
Kelowna	BC	123	May 19	Sept. 20	Sudbury	ON	130	May 17	Sept. 25
Nanaimo	BC	171	Apr. 28	Oct. 17	Thunder Bay	ON	105	Jun. 1	Sept. 15
Nelson	BC	159	May 4	Oct. 13	Timmins	ON	89	Jun. 8	Sept. 6
Port Alberni	BC	159	May 8	Oct. 15	Toronto	ON	149	May 9	Oct. 6
Prince George	BC	91	Jun. 4	Sept. 3	Windsor	ON	179	Apr. 25	Oct. 22
Prince Rupert	BC	156	May 9	Oct. 13	Charlottetown	PE	150	May 17	Oct. 14
Vancouver	BC	221	Mar. 28	Nov. 5	Summerside	PE	162	May 9	Oct. 19
Victoria	BC	200	Apr. 19	Nov. 5	Tignish	PE	138	May 23	Oct. 9
Brandon	MB	105	May 27	Sept. 10	Baie Comeau	QC	109	May 28	Sept. 15
Lynn Lake	MB	89	Jun. 8	Sept. 6	Chicoutimi	QC	133	May 17	Sept. 30
The Pas	MB	112	May 27	Sept. 17	Montreal	QC	156	May 3	Oct. 7
Thompson	MB	61	Jun. 15	Aug. 16	Quebec	QC	139	May 13	Sept. 29
Winnipeg	MB	119	May 25	Sept. 22	Rimouski	QC	139	May 13	Sept. 30
Bathurst	NB	129	May 19	Sept. 26	Sherbrooke	QC	100	Jun. 1	Sept. 10
Edmundston	NB	112	May 28	Sept. 18	Tadoussac	QC	141	May 13	Oct. 2
Fredericton	NB	124	May 20	Sept. 22	Thetford Mines	QC	106	May 28	Sept. 14
Moncton	NB	125	May 24	Sept. 27	Trois-Rivieres	QC	124	May 19	Sept. 23
Saint John	NB	139	May 18	Oct. 4	Moose Jaw	SK	120	May 20	Sept. 18
Corner Brook	NF	142	May 22	Oct. 12	North Battleford	SK	120	May 19	Sept. 17
Gander	NF	123	Jun. 3	Oct. 5	Prince Albert	SK	93	Jun. 2	Sept. 4
Grand Falls	NF	115	Jun. 2	Sept. 26	Regina	SK	111	May 21	Sept. 10
St. John's	NF	131	Jun. 2	Oct. 12	Saskatoon	SK	116	May 21	Sept. 15
Halifax	NS	166	May 6	Oct. 20	Weyburn	SK	112	May 22	Sept. 12
Kentville	NS	141	May 16	Oct. 5	Yorkton	SK	110	May 23	Sept. 11
Sydney	NS	141	May 24	Oct. 13	Dawson	YT	62	Jun. 13	Aug. 17
Truro	NS	113	May 30	Sept. 21	Watson Lake	YT	91	Jun. 2	Sept. 4
Yarmouth	NS	169	May 1	Oct. 18					

(Courtesy of Environment Canada)

Seed germination is a critical time for moisture, but not too much!

To get a jump on growing hot crops, start the seeds indoors or buy seedlings or small plants for transplanting.

COOL VS. HOT CROPS

Whether a crop is "cool," "warm" or "hot" tells you at what point in the season it is planted. Cool crops, such as spinach, leaf lettuce, mustard greens and radishes, may be planted as soon as the soil can be worked in early spring. Because these vegetables germinate and mature quickly, they can be either re-sown or replaced by a warm or hot crop. Cool crops dislike the hot weather of midsummer, but can be planted again in the cooler temperatures of fall.

All the cool crops that I recommend for early planting are frost-tolerant to a degree but they can rot in the ground if you experience a long, cold, wet spring. If your spring weather is very slow in coming, protect your plants with thermal blankets, cloches, a floating row cover or other devices (even an upside-down milk bottle can help a lot) until the earth warms up.

Warm, relatively quick-growing crops such as cabbage, cauliflower, broccoli, Brussels sprouts, endive, escarole and collard greens should be planted no sooner than one or two weeks after the last frost date. Hot crops like beans, peppers, tomatoes, corn and all of the melon or pumpkin family can be planted only once the air and the soil are warm (i.e., above 20°C). They can replace any cool crop that matures relatively quickly.

Corn, carrots, beets and parsley are slow growing and will keep the ground occupied for most of the season—beets for eight weeks, carrots for about three months.

Many vegetables have early, middle and late varieties that can be sown and that mature at different points of the season. Check out the seed packets at your retailer or your favourite seed catalogues carefully for the number of days to maturity.

Experiment with your vegetable patch, but if your space and the time are limited, choose quick-maturing vegetables from the cool and warm groups such as lettuce, radishes, peas or beans.

Beans grow best from seed sown directly in the garden.

A transparent cloche protects a young seedling after planting and hastens maturity.

After seeding directly in the garden, I "mark my row" with vermiculite, or sharp sand.

SOWING SEEDS

Whether starting seeds indoors or planting directly outside, the rule of thumb is that seeds should be sown to a depth equivalent to two to three times their diameter. Very tiny seeds can be pressed lightly into the soil with a finger or can be spread lightly and then covered with a little soil.

If planting directly outdoors, create a furrow with a stick, trowel or hoe tip to the appropriate depth for the seeds, distribute the seeds, then fill in the furrow.

Small seeds that stick together can be mixed with a little talcum powder to stop them from doing so. To sow very tiny seeds, I mix about three parts of sand to one part seed. The sand mixture is then dribbled into the furrows, or distributed into the holes.

I like to pour a thin layer of dried sand or vermiculite over the seeded row to mark it. This way I have a reminder of where the rows are located, and it also minimizes weeding early in the season.

All seeds must be kept in moist soil until they sprout. For seeds started indoors, mist the surface of the soil so it doesn't crust over. Be sure to plant out just as soon as the seeds have sprouted. This works best for large seeded vegetables like beans.

HARDENING OFF SEEDLINGS

If seeds have been started indoors, they will need to be hardened off for a week or two before they are transplanted. Hardening off prepares the tender seedlings for the rise and fall of temperature and moisture levels outside. Put your seedlings in a shaded spot outside, protected from the wind and harsh elements, for a couple of hours and then return them indoors. Each day, leave them out for a little longer, until they can cope with outdoor conditions, then transplant them.

Keep them well watered and well fed with nutrient-rich compost and plenty of sunlight—healthy plants are always more resistant to disease and pests.

DEALING WITH PESTS

Inspect the plants regularly and get rid of pests as soon as you see them so they don't multiply. If you spot only a few interlopers, pick them off and destroy them. If you are dealing with an infestation, use ladybugs and other natural predators. Along with the vegetables, grow flowers to attract beneficial insects; and create a habitat for birds—they are an excellent pest control.

If an insect problem is persistent, use insecticidal soap or a pyrethrin-based natural insecticide like Green Earth AIM. If you have a slug problem, encourage toads to your garden: they have voracious appetites for the slimy beasts. I also find diatomaceous earth effective for controlling slugs and Colorado potato beetles.

If you need more help identifying pests or finding solutions, consult your local garden centre or check out www.markcullen.com where you will find many answers to your gardening problems and links to helpful websites.

A large garden requires a large composter.

HARVESTING CROPS

Crops that favour warm or hot weather have to be harvested before fall frost damages them. Tomatoes and squash will stop growing at 13°C, while lettuce stops at 4.5°C and spinach not until 2°C.

Many cool crops can withstand frost, but they will stop growing once the temperature drops significantly. Beets, carrots, leeks and parsnips can be left in the ground over the winter if they're under a heavy mulch of hay or straw.

After harvest, either remove all remaining plant material from the beds and put it in the compost bin or just bury pest- and disease-free plants in the soil. The leaves and stems will rot down by planting time next spring, making good earthworm fodder.

I compost all my tomato plants and other finished vegetables after a killing frost. Even if they have some mold on them, I find that the heat of the composting-decomposing process takes care of it.

THE IMPORTANCE OF CROP ROTATION

I have found the majority of farmers, as stewards of our largest inhabited tracts of land, are very conscious of the impact their practices have on the environment. One long-standing farming principle that we can use to our advantage in the home garden is crop rotation.

Plants, both vegetable and ornamental, in the same family tend to be vulnerable to the same insects and diseases. Certain families, such as cabbage and potato, are especially at risk for soil-borne predators. So keeping plants from the same family in separate beds one year, and relocating those plants to entirely new beds the following year, may save the vegetables from predation, and you from heartache.

What's more, rotating crops helps to keep the soil fertile by allowing light feeders to occupy soil depleted by heavy feeders while additions of compost or other organic material replenish the nutrients.

Plant families can be large, however, and often hold surprises. It's hard to believe that the earthy, lumpy potato is related to the graceful Chinese lantern, but there you are. When planning your vegetable garden, check the chart on the next page so that you don't have family members side by side or growing in the bed their cousins called home last year.

CROP ROTATION

PLANT FAMILY	VEGETABLES & HERBS	ORNAMENTAL	ROTATION
Apiaceae (Umbelliferae) (Parsley)	**Heavy feeders:** celery, celeriac **Light feeders:** carrot, parsnips, parsley, dill, fennel, lovage (perennial), chervil, caraway, anise, coriander		Interplant and rotate with leafy or fruiting crops of other families—lettuce and tomatoes, for example. These are deep-rooted plants that help break up soil.
Asteraceae (Compositae) (Sunflower)	**Medium feeders:** lettuce **Light feeders:** salsify, chicory, dandelion, yarrow, chamomile, perennial tarragon, globe and Jerusalem artichokes, sunflowers, endive, cardoon	Daisies, zinnias, dahlias, marigolds, asters, chrysanthemums	Rotate leafy Asteraceae plants with Apiaceae, Cucurbitaceae, Fabaceae, Liliaceae, Solanaceae. Alternate sunflowers with tall or staked plants like peas or pole beans. Jerusalem artichokes are perennial—no rotation. Rotate marigolds with tomatoes.
Brassicaceae (Cruciferae) (Mustard)	**Heavy feeders:** cabbage, cauliflower, Chinese cabbage, mustard greens, cress, watercress, horseradish (perennial) **Medium feeders:** broccoli, Brussels sprouts, kale, kohlrabi, rutabaga, turnip **Light feeders:** radish	Sweet alyssum, arabis, aubrieta, aurinia, ornamental kale and cabbage, evening stock, Virginia stock, candytuft, wallflower	
Chenopodiaceae (Beet)	**Medium feeders:** Swiss chard, spinach **Light feeders:** beet		Rotate with Brassicaceae, Fabaceae, Liliaceae, Solanaceae.
Convolvulaceae (Morning glory)	**Light feeders:** sweet potatoes	Morning glories	Rotate morning glories with pole beans, beans, Cucurbitaceae.
Cucurbitaceae (Gourd)	**Heavy feeders:** summer and winter squash, pumpkins, melons, cucumbers, gourds		When staked, rotate with other staked or climbing plants, pole beans, sunflowers, beans. If spreading, rotate with potatoes or leafy Asteraceae.
Fabaceae (Leguminosae) (Pea)	**Medium feeders:** beans, peas, lentils	Sweet peas, lupines	Can be left unrotated for years, but if turned under before fruiting, they add nitrogen to the soil so can improve the soil for plants that follow them.
Liliaceae (Lily)	**Heavy feeders:** asparagus (perennial) **Medium feeders:** leeks **Light feeders:** onions, garlic, shallots, chives (perennial)	Lilies (perennial)	Onions and other perennials in this family do not need to be rotated; they have few pests and can be interplanted with other families to discourage pests from neighbouring beds.
Poaceae (Gramineae) (Corn)	**Heavy feeder:** corn	Some ornamental grasses	Rotate with legumes (corn is a very heavy consumer of soil nutrients).
Solanaceae (Nightshade)	**Medium feeders:** eggplant, peppers **Light feeders:** garden huckleberries, ground cherries, tomatillos	Petunia, nicotiana, schizanthus, nierembergia, physalis, Chinese lantern	Vulnerable to fungus diseases and nematodes; members should be kept separate; rotate with plants of similar size and height from other families.

Young beets.

Pre-thinned beets.

Ready to pull and eat.

SUCCESSION PLANTING

Succession planting is the practice of re-sowing the garden as you harvest. By putting a little thought into what to plant when, you can keep your garden full of good things to eat right through the fall.

You can also interplant vegetables with flowers in your beds: once you harvest all that wonderful spinach late in spring or early summer, you are going to have a bare spot. Do you want to replace it with some annual flowers or plant another vegetable that will grow well through the height of the summer?

MICROCLIMATES - YOUR SECRET WEAPON

Microclimates are areas in your garden that are protected from prevailing winds and take advantage of radiant heat from fences and walls. These special areas provide an opportunity to grow vegetables earlier than you might otherwise and, in some cases, to experiment with crops that you may not be able to grow in more exposed areas.

HOW TO CREATE MICROCLIMATES

Lay down light-coloured coverings such as a white landscape fabric or floating row cover to reflect the sun. Avoid low-lying areas of the garden (these are frost pockets that will also be cooler all summer long). Amend your soil well and consider using containers or raised beds to capture as much heat and sun as possible. Plant a hedge or build a fence on the west and north side of your garden to stop damage from prevailing westerly winds.

COOL CROPS PLANT THESE IN EARLY SPRING OR LATE SUMMER

BEETS
(Beta vulgaris)

With their deep green, red-veined leaves, beets can be a pretty addition to any garden and are easy to grow direct from seed. The tops are edible as well as the beets—pick the greens, which are full of vitamins, early in the season for the best flavour. Early or late canning and bunching varieties are now available in red, white and yellow, in a number of sizes. Beets grow well with carrots, cucumbers, onions and lettuce.

DAYS TO HARVEST

From planting to harvest: 50 to 60 days. Plant as soon as the soil can be worked in early spring. Beets are frost-tolerant. Plant at intervals until about 10 weeks before hard frost is predicted. Do not sow beets in midsummer when the intense heat will damage the seedlings. They must be harvested before the root becomes woody and inedible.

SOIL REQUIREMENTS

Beets like a rich, sandy loam. Amend the soil with compost or well-rotted manure, along with some blood and bone meal to ensure it is fertile and well-drained. The pH should be 6.5 to 7.5. Beets require a consistent source of water but don't overwater, as this can cause excessive leaf growth and small roots.

SPACING

Plant seeds to a depth of 1.5 centimetres (half an inch) in spring, 2.5 centimetres (one inch) in summer, and space them three to five centimetres (one to two inches) apart. Since each seed sprouts several beets, thin to 2.5 centimetres (one inch) apart once the beets are five centimetres (two inches) tall. Thin again to 7.5 centimetres (three inches) when they reach 10 centimetres (four inches). Larger winter-keeper types need to be thinned even more.

A broccoli side shoot.

BROCCOLI
(Brassica oleracea)

One of North America's favourite vegetables, broccoli is available in a wide variety of types including early and late ones, and some different colours such as purple. Broccoli grows well with onions, garlic, beets and chards.

DAYS TO HARVEST

From planting to harvest: 60 to 85 days when planting transplants.

Plant broccoli transplants about two weeks *before* the last expected spring frost. Depending on the length of your growing season, you can plant successive crops through July for fall harvest. Cut when the heads have formed, well before the flowers open. Once you have harvested the main head, smaller side shoots will appear and can be harvested as well. Pick broccoli by cutting the stem just above where leaves join it. Mature broccoli can survive a light frost.

Broccoli is a large plant so give it lots of space.

SOIL REQUIREMENTS

Broccoli is quite easy to grow, but unlike many other vegetables, it does not do well in slightly acidic soil where it is susceptible to disease. If your soil is naturally acidic, add sharp sand and horticultural limestone to raise the pH to an acceptable level. Broccoli is a heavy feeder that likes a nitrogen-rich soil, so fertilize with well-rotted manure at planting time. Keep the plants well watered, as broccoli has shallow roots and can dry out easily. It also tends to bolt to seed in the heat of the summer. Prevent this by harvesting it often.

SPACING

You'll have the best results from planting transplants, but if you do direct sow, sow two or three seeds six millimetres (1/4 inch) deep at 60 centimetre (two-foot) intervals. Thin out all but the hardiest shoots when five centimetres (two inches) tall.

CARROTS
(Daucus carota)

Fast-growing weeds can choke out carrot seedlings so weed thoroughly starting early in the season. Water at least once a week and more than that in the first few weeks and during hot weather. Carrots grow well with lettuce, radishes and tomatoes.

DAYS TO HARVEST

From planting to harvest: 60 to 80 days. Sow seeds *up to four weeks before* last frost (as soon as the soil can be worked). I recommend that you intensely sow seeds in blocks, rather than in rows and thin the crop aggressively if they are growing too closely together. Spacing should be about five centimetres (two inches) apart if you are going to allow each carrot plant to grow to maturity.

Re-sow every three weeks until about 60 days before hard frost is expected, for a succession of crops. Begin to harvest carrots when you can see the orange tops at the base of the leaves. If you want to pick only

at full size, wait until the visible tops are about two centimetres (3/4 of an inch) wide, but small young carrots are especially delicious. While frost may damage the tops, the carrots themselves can withstand it, so you can "store" carrots in the ground right up to the point that it freezes solid.

SOIL REQUIREMENTS

Carrots like light, friable soil that is stone-free. Work the soil to a depth of 20 to 25 centimetres (eight to 10 inches). Heavy, compacted or rocky soil will produce stunted, misshapen or split carrots. Top-dress with mature compost at mid-season. Dig in plenty of well-rotted organic matter in the fall. Keep the soil moist to avoid root splitting and bolting.

SPACING

Sow seeds 1 cm (about 1/2 inch) deep and about five centimetres (two inches) apart or scatter seed across a 15- to 20-centimetre (six- to eight-inch) width.

Dig carrots with a garden fork to minimize damage to roots.

Harvest leaf lettuce frequently to keep it producing.

There are many varieties of lettuce to choose from, including some extremely decorative ones that wouldn't be out of place in an ornamental border. For a longer harvest, look for slow-bolting varieties: the leaves turn bitter after bolting occurs.

LETTUCE
(*Lactuca sativa*)

Lettuce grows well with cucumbers, onions, radishes and carrots.

DAYS TO HARVEST

From planting to harvest: loose leaf—40 to 60 days; butterheads—60 to 75 days; romaine—75 days; iceberg and other crisphead varieties—90 days. Sow seeds as soon as the earth can be worked in the spring. For continual harvest, sow only as much as your family will consume in a week, but sow new seeds every week, from the second week of April until mid-May in most parts of the country (earlier in coastal BC).

Since lettuce that matures in hot weather bolts quickly, skip a few weeks of sowing from mid May through July or plant only slow-bolting varieties in June and early July. As the lettuce plants mature, pick the outer leaves for immediate use. Harvest romaine lettuce by cutting it at the base when it is about 30 centimetres (12 inches) in diameter; butterhead when it is 25 centimetres (10 inches) in diameter.

SOIL REQUIREMENTS

Lettuce likes neutral to slightly acidic soil that is moisture-retentive and rich in organic material. It prefers an open, sunny site.

SPACING

Leaf lettuce can be planted closely; head lettuce should be thinned to 20 to 25 centimetres (eight to 10 inches) apart.

Look for slow-bolting varieties of lettuce.

Onions are ready for harvest when the tops fall over.

ONIONS AND LEEKS
(*Allium cepa*)

Consider planting a few different varieties of onions in your garden. They are easy to grow, very space efficient, and many types are quite attractive. Hardy perennial onions include bunching or Welsh onions and Egyptian onions. Leeks are best grown from seedling stage rather than direct seeded.

Onions can be grown from seeds or "sets" (small bulbs). Gardeners with short growing seasons will want to use sets or start seeds indoors in February to guarantee a good harvest. Shallots are difficult to grow from seed; I recommend that you use sets instead. Sow seeds or sets as soon as the soil can be worked.

DAYS TO HARVEST

From planting to harvest: 90 to 120 days (from sets); 65 days (from transplants). You will know that your onions are ready for use when the tops droop over on their own. Harvest by pulling green onions out of the soil as you need them; dig up large onions when the tops turn yellow. Dry large onions in the sun for two days before storing them in a cool, dry place to prevent rotting.

SOIL REQUIREMENTS

Soil should be rich and well drained. Regular watering and weeding are needed for good growth; adding compost in mid-season is also a good idea.

SPACING

Seeds should be spaced 13 mm (1/2 inch) apart; sets should be spaced 13 to 20 centimetres (five to eight inches) apart with their tops crowning at or just above the soil surface. Large onions should be thinned when stocks are 20 centimetres (eight inches) tall by removing every second onion (*eat these*). Thin globe and Spanish onions three times before harvesting.

Cold-hardy leeks taste best after several frosts.

Young Spanish onions. They can be eaten any time through maturity.

Snow peas ready for harvest.

PEAS - SHELL, SNAP AND SNOW PEAS
(*Pisum sativum*)

Most pea varieties (with the exception of dwarf varieties) need to be grown against a trellis, fence, chicken wire or other support. Direct sow for best results. Peas grow well with other legumes, root crops, potatoes, cucurbits and corn.

Give your snow peas rich, slightly acidic soil.

DAYS TO HARVEST

From planting to harvest: 55 to 80 days. Sow seeds as soon as the soil can be worked. Peas like long cool days and can withstand frost, so plant early in the spring or late in the season for a fall harvest. Pea plants stop producing fruit when the temperature rises above 24°C. You can either choose peas with different maturity dates and plant all at the same time, or sow another planting three or four weeks after the initial spring sowing to prolong your summer harvest. Pick regularly so the peas don't get tough. Shelling peas and snap peas are harvested when the pods are rounded and plump; snow peas are picked when the pods are still flat.

SOIL REQUIREMENTS

Peas like rich, slightly acidic soil. They prefer moist soil, so water deeply in dry weather. Peas are medium feeders, but will produce more foliage than fruit if the soil is very nitrogen-rich. Side-dress the beds with compost when the plants are 15 to 25 centimetres (six to 10 inches) tall.

SPACING

Set seeds about 2.5 centimetres (one inch) deep, five centimetres (two inches) apart.

Young spinach leaves.

SPINACH
(Spinacia oleracea)

Spinach thrives in cool temperatures. It does not grow well in hot weather which causes bolting to seed quickly. It is slow to germinate so I recommend that you use transplants. Spinach likes full sun to partial shade. For best results, grow spinach with beans, peas, corn and strawberries.

DAYS TO HARVEST

From planting to harvest from transplant: 40 to 60 days. Plant seedlings as soon as the soil can be worked and every three weeks after that until the daytime temperatures become a consistent 21°C. After that, it will bolt to seed. Resume planting in July through to six weeks before first frost (it will overwinter and reappear in the spring). Pick individual leaves to prolong the harvest.

SOIL REQUIREMENTS

Spinach likes average to rich, well-drained soil with a neutral pH. Dig in well-rotted organic matter before planting. On poor soils, leaves are stunted, bitter, and prone to bolt. Never allow the soil to dry out completely.

SPACING

Sow seeds 1.5 centimetres (1/2 inch) deep in furrows 35 centimetres (14 inches) apart.

Spinach grows best in cool temperatures.

Runner beans—doing what they do best—running!

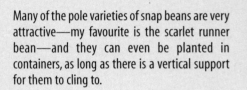

Many of the pole varieties of snap beans are very attractive—my favourite is the scarlet runner bean—and they can even be planted in containers, as long as there is a vertical support for them to cling to.

WARM CROPS

These should only be planted after all threat of frost is past.

SNAP BEANS
(Phaseolus vulgaris)
Snap beans, also called string beans, green beans or wax beans, are easy to grow and an excellent vegetable for those short on space. Direct sow from seed.

DAYS TO HARVEST
From planting to harvest: pole varieties—60 to 70 days; bush varieties—45 to 60 days. Sow seeds outdoors just before the last frost until about mid-June. Pick beans when pencil-thick (they will toughen if left to grow any thicker). During the harvesting period (about three weeks) this will probably mean checking your plants every two or three days. Pick large tough beans that you've missed so that new beans will be produced. Add older beans to the compost bin—they are full of nitrogen.

SOIL REQUIREMENTS
Snap beans need no special soil preparation, providing the soil is friable, but they will not germinate

Do not pick beans while plants are wet.

until the soil reaches 16°C or warmer. Water regularly, especially during and immediately after flowering and once pods have appeared. Beans are medium feeders, so give them a side-dressing of mature compost when they get about 15 centimetres (six inches) tall.

SPACING
Pole varieties or climbing beans can be grown up a trellis, string or pole that stands at least two metres (six feet) tall. Bush beans do not need to be supported but require a bit more room to accommodate their spread. Place seeds about 2.5 centimetres (one inch) deep and 2.5 to 3.5 centimetres (one to 1 1/2 inches) apart for bush beans; five to six seeds around the pole or string for pole beans.

Keep picking ripe beans to encourage flowering and further fruiting.

Cucumbers forming; they mature in 50 to 70 days.

There is a wide variety of cucumbers including lemon, white and long gourmet cucumbers. "Burpless" cucumbers are the mildest and thinnest skinned. Vining cucumbers are grown vertically on uprights (like pole beans), but the fruit may need to be supported by cloth slings or netting due to its weight. Compact varieties such as 'Patio Pic' work very well in containers.

CUCUMBER
(Cucumis sativus)
DAYS TO HARVEST

From planting to harvest: 50 to 70 days. Plant out seedlings that have been started indoors once all danger of frost has passed. Harvest pickling cucumbers when they've reached about 7.5 centimetres (three inches) in length, slicing varieties when 15 centimetres (six inches) long, and the English seedless type at 35 centimetres (14 inches) or longer. All should be picked before they turn yellow. Always remove ripe or overripe cucumbers to encourage the plant to produce more fruit.

SOIL REQUIREMENTS

Cucumbers need good air circulation and well-drained soil. Before planting, prepare a hole 15 centimetres (six inches) deep and 60 centimetres (two feet) in diameter and fill with well-rotted manure. Mix a shovelful of compost with the soil you removed from the hole. Mound this soil over the hole, covering the manure. After planting, mulch with clean straw or fine pine/cedar bark. Keep cucumbers well watered (never allow plants to wilt from dehydration).

SPACING

Plant three to five seeds, 2.5 to five centimetres (one to two inches) deep, in each hill of soil. Space hills two metres (six feet) apart.

ZUCCHINI
(Cucurbita pepo)

Zucchini is the most popular of the summer squashes, and it is very easy to grow, providing that you have the sunshine and heat to bring them to maturity. Direct seed in mounds, putting three or four seeds in each mound. Keep in mind that one plant produces about 16 fruit and that zucchini does not store very well. Depending on the size of your family and the number of zucchini recipes you have, one or two plants may be all you need.

DAYS TO HARVEST

From planting to harvest: 50 to 60 days. Sow seeds one to 2.5 centimetres (1/4 to one inch) deep about a week after the last frost date. Zucchini can grow to enormous sizes but the flavour and texture are much better when the vegetables are quite small—10 to 15 centimetres (four to six inches) long. Picking them early also encourages the plant to produce more. Harvest all zucchinis before they are damaged by frost.

Zucchini, Cucumber and Squash are "open pollinated," requiring bees or other pollinators to ensure optimum production.

SOIL REQUIREMENTS

Zucchini like warm, rich, well-drained soil and a sunny spot protected from wind. Water deeply once a week, especially during dry spells.

SPACING

If planting more than one zucchini bush, plant seeds 15 centimetres (six inches) apart and thin plants so they are 30 centimetres (one foot) apart.

Zucchini flowers are rich in folic acid and delicious when battered and fried, or simply dusted with flower and sautéed.

Pepper flower.

PEPPERS
(Capsicum annuum)

There just can't be too much sun for pepper plants. They like about eight hours of full sun a day and lots of heat. If your peppers don't look like much by midsummer, don't panic—they will fill out very quickly in the second half of the season. Plant transplants for best results.

SOIL REQUIREMENTS

Peppers like warm, loose, well-drained soil. Consistent, generous watering is important for good growth—give them a good soaking twice a week or as the soil becomes dry past the top two centimetres (3/4 inch). If the soil is not nutrient-rich, add blood and bone meal to the surface of the soil once a month.

SPACING

Sweet pepper plants should be spaced 20 to 30 centimetres (eight to 12 inches) apart, while hot peppers need 35 to 45 centimetres (14 to 18 inches) between them as they tend to grow wider.

DAYS TO HARVEST

From planting to harvest: 60 to 80 days (from transplants). Seeds should be started indoors about 10 weeks before the last frost, but you may want to purchase small plants from their garden centre to get a good head start.

Set transplants outside when the weather and soil are warm and all danger of frost is long gone. Pinch off the bottom leaves and set the plants a little lower in the soil than they were sitting in the pot to encourage new root growth. Harvest peppers frequently to encourage more fruit production.

Unlike tomatoes, peppers keep quite well on the plant, giving you a long harvest time.

TOMATOES
(*Lycopersicon esculentum*)

Tomatoes are the most popular garden vegetable in Canada by far, for two reasons—they are easy to grow just about anywhere there is heat and sun (with apologies to my friends in Newfoundland and on the BC coast) and they taste so much better fresh from your own vine than the supermarket ones that are strip-mined in some remote place.

The two basic types of tomatoes are bush tomatoes (often referred to as "determinate" varieties) and staking varieties (called "indeterminate"). The former are generally grown in tomato cages or on a tomato spiral and produce fruit in a concentrated period of time. Indeterminate varieties need to be supported on a pole or trellis and bear fruit progressively over the growing season. These types need to be pruned.

There is a huge variety of tomatoes to choose from, in colours ranging from white, yellow and orange to pink, red, green and purple, and in sizes from huge beefsteak types to tiny grape tomatoes. You can find early and mid-season varieties; plum tomatoes that are ideal for paste and sauce; tomatoes that are disease-resistant; and even "square" tomatoes that won't roll off the table! My favourites include 'Sweet Million' cherry tomatoes, which work very well in containers; 'Whopper', a good medium-sized, disease-resistant tomato; and any of the big juicy beefsteak tomatoes.

DAYS TO HARVEST

From planting to harvest: 60 to 80 days. Tomatoes can be started from seed indoors six to eight weeks before the last spring frost. Many gardeners opt for plants from a nursery, but if your have your heart set on a specialty variety, you may have to start with seed instead.

When purchasing seedlings, look for dark glossy leaves and a short, sturdy stem. Put seedlings or transplants into the ground once the temperatures are warm (a minimum of 20°C).

'Early Girl' tomatoes ready to ripen.

Heritage tomatoes generally taste better than commercial types.

throughout the day and night, generally a week after the last frost date. My late friend Lois Hole in St. Albert, AB, recommended taking a chance on an earlier frost date. If you decide to follow suit, be prepared to cover the seedlings with an inverted milk bottle or cloche for protection. Plant the seedlings deep, so the soil comes up to at least their first leaves. New roots will develop along the stem, producing a stronger plant.

SOIL REQUIREMENTS

Tomatoes like plenty of sun—a full eight hours a day, in fact. They also like heat and shelter from the wind. They are heavy feeders so the soil should be rich with organic material at planting time (I can't say enough about compost!). Water at least twice a week, more frequently if the weather is dry and hot.

SPACING

For staking (indeterminate) varieties, space the plants 45 to 60 centimetres (18 to 24 inches) apart and stake within a month after planting to avoid root damage. Set the stake deep in the soil so it is stable, between eight and 13 centimetres away from the plant. As the plant grows, loosely tie it to the stake or use a tomato spiral and simply twist the plant around the metal stake without tying.

For bush (determinate) varieties, leave 90 to 120 centimetres (three to four feet) between plants if you are going to let them sprawl, or 90 centimetres (three feet) between cages.

Prune staking varieties by cutting out suckers growing between the main stem and the branch, as often as twice a week when plants are growing most vigorously.

You can also prune back the top of the stem if it outgrows its stake or at the end of the season when you want the plant to spend its energy on the remaining fruit.

I get more satisfaction from my one-acre vegetable garden than any other part of our 10-acre property. If you have grown vegetables at home, you know what I mean. If you haven't, this is the year to start!

A tomato spiral eliminates the need for tying. All tomatoes benefit from being staked up.

KEY ELEMENT

MARK'S RECIPE FOR TOP TOMATOES
Here is my recipe for the best tomatoes on the block:

1. *Dig a hole the size of a half bushel.*

2. *Fill the hole with a mix of half compost, half topsoil.*

3. *Make a "crater" in the soil and push the young tomato transplant into the soil up to the first set of true leaves.*

4. *Water well and mulch with five centimetres (two inches) of pine/cedar bark or 15 centimetres (six inches) of clean straw.*

5. *Stake with a metal spiral stake (no tying!) during the second half of June.*

6. *Spray with Bordo mixture in July to prevent early blight in August.*

7. *Harvest often—do not allow fruit to rot.*

No garden should be without a pot of fresh herbs.

CHAPTER ELEVEN
Herbs

When we talk of herbs in the garden, we are generally referring to culinary herbs rather than medicinal herbs. This chapter is full of information that will help you enjoy fresh herbs from the garden to the table. Many of the ornamental plants in our garden are technically herbs—including lavender, rosemary and, believe it or not, bananas (though you're unlikely to have a lot of those in your Canadian garden).

Lavender.

Dill flower.

Herbs are indispensable in the kitchen, and it's a lot easier to use basil and parsley on the spur of the moment if you can cut them outside your back door instead of travelling to a local market.

Herbs are also commonly grown in containers, and tender herbs are often brought in to spend the winter on a sunny window ledge. Other herbs are extremely winter-hardy—chives and mint, for example, are perennial to Zone 2.

Generally, herbs need five hours of direct light per day; if you are growing them indoors, place them in south- or west-facing windows, as close to the glass as possible. Most herbs like rich, fertile soil that is neutral in pH. They don't, however, do their best in soils with high nitrogen levels—this reduces the flavour in the leaves and stems. Herbs don't need any supplemental fertilizers during the growing season and, since many popular herbs come from the Mediterranean region, are undemanding where water is concerned.

You can start most herbs from seed, but to get a jump on a short season, many gardeners prefer to buy small plants at their local garden centre. Well-tended perennial herbs can usually be harvested over most of the summer. Start annuals inside and set them out as seedlings when spring arrives. They need to be planted in a well-prepared bed that has been amended with mature compost. Mulches are ideal for keeping in moisture and preventing weeds. Many herbs grow better without chemical fertilizer, which just encourages long, leggy growth.

Rosemary in a container.

Stepping stones in the herb garden.

For a wonderful visual effect, follow ancient traditions and plant herbs in formal patterns around pathways. Many gardeners combine herbs with ornamental flowers in containers and in the garden. Urban gardeners pressed for space often incorporate herbs such as lavender, chives and thyme in their regular flower borders. When bringing plants indoors to winter over, use a well drained potting mix and clean, sterile containers. Trim back plants from time to time, whether you use the cuttings in your cooking or not, an effort to keep the new growth coming.

Herbs are among the oldest cultivated plants, inspiring gardeners for centuries with their flavours and aromatic qualities. They are attractive garden plants, often offering flowers and rich scents.

TOP 10 CANADIAN-GROWN HERBS

BASIL
(Ocimum basilicum)

Eating tomatoes with basil is the best! This annual herb is available in a wide number of varieties including some, like purple basil, that are best known for the colour of their foliage. I have seen them used as shade-loving coleus would be used, except basil loves the sun! It's difficult to grow from seed so most gardeners buy young plants in the spring.

Seedlings are highly susceptible to damping-off, a fungal disease encouraged by wet conditions in seed trays. Prevent this by placing young seedlings in a well-ventilated area or use a small orbital fan to move the air around each plant. Avoid overwatering; allow the surface of the soil to dry between waterings. Plant seedlings outdoors two weeks after the last spring frost in a sheltered spot that receives full sun.

Space the seedlings 30 centimetres (12 inches) apart. Given that basil is fussy about the amount of water it receives, it is a good candidate for containers, where you can monitor the moisture it gets. The soil should be well-drained. Basil is a good companion plant to tomatoes in the garden as well as on the plate, as it repels many flying insects. Pick the young leaves and always harvest from the top of the plant to encourage new growth. Basil will be killed by the first fall frost, so be sure to harvest it all—you can dry it, freeze it or make pesto.

Fresh basil is easy to grow in the garden or containers.

There is nothing easier to grow than chives. I pulled my largest plant out of a friend's compost pile! They're very hardy, too.

CHIVES
(*Allium schoenoprasum*)

Chives are a perennial hardy to Zone 3. With their clusters of purple, mauve, pink or white pompom flowers in June, they are a decorative addition to the garden.

Lift and divide chive clumps every few years in spring. They are easy to grow and can be started from seed, from young plants purchased at a garden centre or from roots taken from a mature plant.

Cilantro.

Plant chives as soon as the soil can be worked (they are wonderfully frost-resistant). They like full sun or light shade and need only average soil. Plant seedlings 18 centimetres (seven inches) apart. Do not allow plants to dry out in summer or the leaves will quickly shrivel. When harvesting chives, you can cut them to within five centimetres (two inches) of the ground four times a year. This helps to maintain a fresh supply of leaves.

Chives grow well in containers on a windowsill, requiring just consistent water and fertilizer to stay green. They are excellent companion plants to roses—many insects, including aphids, hate chives!

CILANTRO
(*Coriandrum sativum*)

Cilantro plants are also called Chinese parsley. The seeds are called coriander.

Cilantro can be seeded directly or grown from young plants. It likes light, well-drained soil that is not nitrogen rich in a location that is sheltered but has full sun. It should be set out only after all danger of frost has passed. Cilantro is difficult to grow in humid weather but thrives in areas with cool evening temperatures.

Space the plants six centimetres (2 1/2 inches) apart if harvesting the leaves. If the goal is to harvest the seeds, then plants should be spaced up to 25 centimetres (10 inches) apart.

You can pick the leaves as soon as they appear (the lower leaves are more flavourful). You may also pick and eat the flowers; even if you don't eat them, you should pinch off the flowers to allow more leaf growth. Seeds should be harvested at the end of the growing season when they are hard and brown.

Cilantro can be grown in containers both indoors on windowsills and outside on patios. The container must have good drainage. Many gardeners find the scent of the cilantro plant to be unpleasant (well-used sweat socks come to mind) and prefer not to grow it indoors.

DILL

(Anethum graveolens)

An annual plant, dill is easy to grow but needs quite a lot of space — it can reach a height of 1.5 metres (five feet) and spread up to 30 centimetres (1 foot).

It likes full sun and will tolerate poor, well-drained soil. In spite of the fact that dill reseeds itself very readily, seedlings are often difficult to transplant, so it is best grown from seed sown directly in the garden. Sow early, approximately at the time of the last spring frost.

In my garden the dill has a habit of re-seeding itself each spring, so I don't have to work very hard at having it in my garden — other than weeding out the plants I don't want. You can use all parts of the dill plant and can begin picking it when it is very young, continuing throughout the growing season. Harvest the

Dill self seeds in the garden. Cull out extra plants as you see fit

flower heads before they open fully. Dill can be grown in containers but does not grow well indoors. Find a sheltered location outdoors that gets full sun.

Aphids can be a problem if the plants are crowded, and slugs love dill plants. But then, so do the beautiful larvae of the swallowtail butterfly. When it comes to plant pests, I pick my spots! Dill is worth the trouble.

WOULD YOU LIKE A MINT?

As a gardener you may want to consider this question carefully before you answer! Truth is, the family of mints is huge — there are 25 species in the genus of *Mentha* and many hundreds of genera.

Mints can be fabulous mimics (much like scented geraniums) and it might surprise you how many mints look like mint but smell like something else. Take apple mint, for instance, or pineapple mint (*Mentha suaveolens*).

Members of the mint family are characterized by their square stems.

MORE MINTS

I'm not suggesting you attempt to fool your dinner guests but try adding a few apple mint leaves to your next apple pie and see what they say.

Your cat enjoys mint… cat mint, of course (Nepeta faassenii). You can start this aggressive plant very easily from seed or buy the transplants from the nursery in the spring. Cats do tend to make a mess of established plants. I put short bamboo stakes into the soil at their base to discourage too much beating amongst the bushes here. Seems to work.

By the way, not all mints are famous for their flavour. Orange or bergamot mint (Mentha citrata) is a very popular native perennial plant in many parts of Canada and it's a magnet for hummingbirds and butterflies.

MINT

(*Mentha*)

Hardy to Zone 4, mint is easy to grow and comes in many varieties from peppermint and spearmint to lemon and ginger. Its only drawback is that it is highly invasive.

Growing it in a large pot or container is probably the only way to save your flower beds from being overrun. If you grow it in the garden, plant it in a large metal coffee tin set halfway into the soil, with the bottom cut out of it. But keep your eye on it — mint can actually "jump" out of this tin.

Best started with young plants from a garden centre or from plant division, mint prefers some shade but can tolerate full sun. It likes moist, rich soil, but isn't overly fussy. Just keep it 60 to 90 centimetres (two to three feet) away from other plants. Mint requires regular watering and individual leaves can be picked at any time or the whole plant can be cut down to 10 centimetres (four inches) twice during the season.

Most varieties of mint (ginger mint, buddleja mint, peppermint, lemon mint and spearmint) are hardy to Zone 5 but should be protected by a good snow cover. After three or four years, mint plants become woody and should be replaced. You can rejuvenate the original plant by taking rooted plantlets from the outside growth of the mature plant.

Spearmint and peppermint will help deter aphids when planted near roses.

Mint also attracts bees and butterflies and is an excellent companion plant with cabbages and tomatoes.

Edible flower salad.

FENNEL
(*Foeniculum vulgare*)

Hardy to Zone 6, fennel is often grown for its ornamental yellow flowers that attract butterflies and bees. The blooms are edible if eaten before they actually open. More commonly used are the leaves, which taste like licorice. Fennel reaches maturity in 80 days and produces seeds several weeks later. The seeds contain an oil that produces an allergic reaction in some people who touch them. This herb is easy to grow in a location with full sun. Soil should be well-drained; rich deep soil produces tender foliage. Plants can grow 90 to 120 centimetres (three to four feet) in height and, in windy locations, may require staking.

FLOWERS WITH EDIBLE PETALS

- Apple blossoms
- Snap bean blossoms
- Bergamot
- Borage
- Calendula
- Chive blossoms
- Chrysanthemum
- Clover
- Fuchsia
- Geranium
- Gladiolus
- Hibiscus
- Hollyhock
- Impatiens
- Jasmine
- Lavender
- Lilac
- Lily (including daylily)
- Mallow
- Marigold
- Nasturtium
- Orange blossoms
- Pansies
- Pea
- Primrose
- Rose
- Saffron crocus
- Snapdragon
- Sunflower
- Tulip
- Squash
- Viola
- Violets

Fennel.

THYME
(*Thymus*)

A huge assortment of thymes is available in all sorts of flavours and colours, some perennial and some annual. Most perennial varieties are hardy to Zone 5 with winter protection, and can make a very attractive ornamental groundcover as well.

Thyme can be grown from seed but is easiest from young plants. Set out as soon as the soil can be worked (it can tolerate light frost). Thyme likes full sun and light, well-drained soil though it will tolerate poor soil. It doesn't like to dry out. However, overwatering and too much fertilizer will produce less tasty leaves. The leaves can be picked any time and have more flavour if the flowers are removed (these can be eaten, too). Trim back the plant after it has flowered to promote new growth and stop the plant from becoming woody and spreading out.

All varieties of thyme grow well in containers. Proper drainage is essential and the potting mix should not be too rich or contain fertilizers.

Silver thyme.

Curly parsley.

Lemon Balm.

PARSLEY
(Petroselinum)

Parsley is a tender biennial (that is, it matures in its second year) but can usually be grown as an annual.

Curly or plain leaf parsley varieties are available. (I have seen curly parsley used as a border plant in an ornamental planting and it looked terrific.) Parsley likes moist, average to rich soil. It is easiest to grow from young plants as the seed germinates slowly and only when the soil is quite warm. Plant parsley about a week before the last spring frost date, spacing plants 20 to 25 centimetres (eight to 10 inches) apart. Plants can reach a height of 60 centimetres (two feet) under ideal conditions.

Parsley prefers cool temperatures but will withstand heat quite admirably. It doesn't need a great deal of water, except if planted in containers—then it

When I walk by my rosemary, I always run my fingers through it. Such an appealing scent!

should be watered every day. A good container plant, parsley can be grown indoors as long as it is cut regularly.

While most people like to harvest all their parsley at the end of the season and either dry it or freeze it for future use, I have met gardeners who leave it in the ground and continue to snip the frozen leaves throughout the winter.

ROSEMARY
(Rosmarinus officinalis)

Available in upright as well as trailing forms, rosemary is a perennial in Zone 8 (possibly Zone 7 with protection) but for most gardeners, it is an annual.

However, I have been bringing our rosemary "tree," which now stands about 60 centimetres (two feet) high in a clay pot, indoors to a sunny window for the winter for several years. It provides a wonderful scent of summer especially when we make toasted rosemary bread or just brush against it.

Like parsley, rosemary is often difficult to raise from seed so most gardeners purchase young plants or propagate it from cuttings. Retailers sell a lot of rosemary plants (trimmed like topiaries) around Christmas time. Keep them in a sunny but cool spot and plant outdoors about the time of the last spring frost date.

Rosemary likes poor, well-drained soil and a sunny location. It will tolerate some shade in summer but needs as much sun through the winter as you can give it. Rosemary needs regular

watering only until it is established, after that it is important to let the plant dry significantly between waterings. Overwatering can cause the leaves to drop. Rosemary is well suited to containers; just be sure the potting soil is well-drained. I do not find that fertilizing improves rosemary's performance.

LEMON BALM
(Melissa officinalis)

Hardy to Zone 4 and tough to the point of invasiveness, lemon balm will grow in any degree of light from full sun to full shade. It can be grown from seeds, cuttings or divisions. Given fertile soil and frequent watering, it will reach 60 centimetres (two feet) in height with deep green leaves. It produces small white flowers that attract bees and other pollinators. Harvest lemon balm leaves just before flowers start to form—this is when the fragrance is the strongest.

Shear the plant back to 30 centimetres (one foot) after flowering and it will send out a new flush of foliar growth.

If you are just starting to garden, I encourage you to try some herbs.

If you have been gardening for some time, I urge you to plant more and to experiment with the many herbs that are now available.

While not all plants listed above are technically 'herbs', the truth is the many plants that we refer to as herbs are some of the easiest to grow and most flavourful in the kitchen.

PART THREE
MARK'S RECIPE FOR GARDENING SUCCESS

If you love gardening—I mean doing it, not just looking at it—then at some time or other you also have to love getting your knees dirty.

I find that the more I garden, the more time I want to spend in the garden. Not only does the activity make me feel good but I also learn a lot out there. My mind wanders to places it generally doesn't go otherwise. As I sort out where different plants will go and what job to tackle next, I find myself sorting out many of the things in my life that had been a bit of a jumble.

I feel more relaxed when I come indoors after a day in the garden.

Experienced gardeners share this appreciation for the activity. But much more than that we understand that a garden is a transition between the natural world around us and the world that we have contrived for ourselves indoors. Within square walls with year-round climate control to keep us comfortable, computers, telephones, television and all today's modern gadgetry make up and take up the space that we have constructed for ourselves.

The garden is our halfway point between all of this and the natural world.

This section of my *Canadian Garden Primer* provides the information that you will need to make all of the dirty-knees-days worthwhile.

Have a look through it and you will learn how to make connecting with nature in our gardens a mutually beneficial process. Here are organic techniques that will help you meet your goals for a beautiful garden in earth-friendly ways—and save yourself time and money to boot.

It is, for the most part, practical stuff. But as you will learn through experience, the practical stuff provides its own rewards.

KEY ELEMENT

THE GIFTED GARDENER
An experienced and gifted gardener moved into an old home where an equally old garden had long outlived its previous glory. The new owner got to work and re-created something beautiful from the bones of the old garden.

Some years passed by and he was working in his front yard, with roses and peonies in full blaze on the perfect June day.

The local reverend was walking by and raised a hand to the great gardener, yelling to him, "Good morning. It is a great thing what God and man can do together, isn't it, Bill!"

To which the gardener replied, "It is indeed, pastor—and you should have seen it when God alone was in charge!"

A lush green lawn can find a place even in the organic garden.

CHAPTER TWELVE
Lawn Care

How did a chapter on lawns get into an organic gardening book? The answer is simple: you can enjoy a good-looking lawn while being environmentally responsible and I'm going to tell you how.

A beautiful green lawn complements flower beds and borders, dresses up a

Some Canadian friends share a chat on a beautiful green lawn at the Governor's Mansion, Ohio.

landscape and frames a well-designed garden. Above all, it provides a cool, welcoming carpet of green on a hot day, and offers a soft, durable and oxygen-rich play area for kids. In short, a good looking, well-maintained lawn is the most sophisticated groundcover that I know of. The 9,000 plants in each square metre (10 square feet) of a healthy lawn make it one of the most intensely planted areas of the garden and as such, needs some special care.

The best method of obtaining a weed-free lawn is to produce thick, healthy grass that will shade out weeds and crabgrass, eliminating the need for herbicide.

MARK'S TOP TIPS FOR A HEALTHY LAWN

Here are my 6 steps for producing a thick, healthy, environmentally responsible lawn:

1. Raise your lawn mower cutting height to five to seven centimetres (two to three inches).

2. Use a mulching attachment on your lawn mower to return the nitrogen-rich grass clippings to the soil. Doing this every time you cut your lawn is the equivalent of one fertilizer application to the root zone each season. Mulching does not cause thatch in your lawn!

3. When your lawn is growing actively in spring and fall but not receiving adequate rain to keep it looking green and healthy, I recommend that you apply two to three centimeters (one to 1-1/2 inches) of water once a week rather than watering every day or two. This will establish deeper roots—and the deeper they are, the more drought-resistant your lawn. Water in the morning or late afternoon to minimize evaporation.

4. In the summer, during a drought, do not water. Your lawn will go dormant—not dead. It will turn brown, only to bounce back in cooler, damp weather.

5. Feed with a natural organic fertilizer like compost or well-rotted manure. I will use a slow-release, organic-based nitrogen product like Golfgreen (which is pesticide-free, of course) in the spring and late summer. In the late fall, an organic-based fertilizer specifically formulated for fall is the most important application of the year as this builds up the roots for the long cold Canadian winter ahead.

6. Replace your old power mower with a new one, especially if your old mower is a two-cycle. The new mowers produce far fewer emissions than the old ones. Better still; buy a push-type reel mower. No motor. No emissions. Better exercise. And a nice sound as the blades click on by.

In the face of many municipal bylaw restrictions on the use of garden chemicals, the lawn question I get asked most is: *"How do I control lawn weeds without weed killer?"* The answer is amazingly simple—overseed the thin patches of your lawn each spring with quality grass seed. This is the most effective method of eliminating weeds and improving the overall appearance of the lawn.

HOW TO OVER SEED YOUR LAWN

Overseeding can be done as soon as the ground has dried and is firm enough to walk on. With a spring-tined leaf rake, remove any debris, dead grass, leaves, etc. and add them to your composter.

If your soil is clay-based or your lawn receives high foot traffic, I recommend that you aerate using a power aerator to get the job done quickly. (See "Should I aerate my lawn?" page 132.)

Then spread two to five centimetres (one to two inches) of triple mix over the area, concentrating on the depressions and thin areas.

Sow a good-quality, weed-free, grass seed at a rate of 1 kilo for every 80 square metres (2.2 pounds for every 860 square feet).

The ultimate quality of your lawn will be determined more by the quality of the grass seed that you sow than anything else you do.

Think of the bag of grass seed as containing the pedigree of your future lawn, and buy a premium mix from a reputable retailer. If your lawn is in good shape, simply repair any bare spots and fertilize using compost, well-rotted manure or alfalfa pellets.

REPAIR YOUR LAWN

1. Check lawn for dead patches. (This is snow-mould).

2. Rake patches to remove debris and dead grass.

3. Spread a layer of triple mix 1 to 2 centimetres thick.

4. Sow grass seed and keep moist until seed germinates.

SHOULD I DETHATCH MY LAWN?

Thatch is the layer of organic material that builds up between soil and green vegetation, and may exist uniformly across an entire lawn or appear in spots. It is a tightly woven layer of both living and dead leaves, roots and stems that, in a limited accumulation of up to 1.5 centimetres (about 1/2 inch), protects the roots and insulates the soil, resulting in a more weed-free, drought-tolerant lawn with vibrant colour and strengthened stress tolerance.

However, a thicker (more than 1.5 centimetres) layer of thatch can reduce water filtration, lower drought tolerance, interfere with nutrients moving to the root zone, and hinder overseeding. Grass plants deprived of air, nutrients and moisture will become unhealthy and prone to insects and disease. Thatch accumulates wherever decomposition falls short of the rate at which grass plants are produced. In other words, thatch is only a problem at certain times of year (usually spring) and only in some growing areas— usually where soil is clay based, poorly draining and when there is a preponderance of rainfall.

Excess thatch can happen when any or all of the following conditions are present:

• *Poor drainage.* When the large pore spaces in the soil remain filled with water, soil microorganisms receive less oxygen.

"Plug" from aerator.

Pull back grass blades to examine the thatch. If it's thicker than 1.5 centimetres (1/2inch), it should be raked out.

• *Overwatering.* Waterlogged pore spaces result in less oxygen being diffused into the soil.

• *Compacted soil.* If the soil is insufficiently aerated, the microorganism activity that will degrade thatch slows down.

• *High nitrogen fertility.* If grass plant parts are being produced more quickly than old dead parts are decomposing, thatch occurs.

• *Vigorous turf grass.* Certain cultivars such as Kentucky bluegrass produce thatch readily.

To check your thatch layer, cut a core about eight centimetres (three inches) deep and examine it.

If the thatch is more than 1.5 centimetres (about 1/2 inch) thick, you should take action. Reduce thatch by applying compost to increase microorganism activity, or by removing enough thatch so the crowns of the grass plants develop at the soil surface once again.

Use a dethatching rake or rent a mechanical dethatcher (a machine that cuts through the thatch and lifts it to the surface). Rake up the thatch and add it to your compost.

Thatch buildup cannot entirely be prevented. However, you can slow the buildup if you encourage grass roots to grow deeply into the soil. Cut the grass to a height of six to eight centimetres, water deeply and aerate. Reduce the frequency and amount of irrigation so that less water remains in soil pores. Rake the lawn vigorously in the spring and work compost into the thatch layer to help it decompose. Dethatching every three to five years should be plenty.

Thatch rake.

I like to use a manual aerator on areas of my lawn that receive a lot of foot traffic. For instance, the path that the mail carrier takes across my front lawn, is the perfect place to "open up the soil" each spring with a manual aerator.

LAWN AERATION

SHOULD I AERATE MY LAWN?

Heavy clay soils benefit from aeration every three or four years. Over time, the soil becomes compacted, making it difficult for air to enter. Use an aerator to open up the soil and allow the lawn to breath. Aerators have sharpened tubes that lift up plugs of earth, leaving little holes about one centimetre (just over 1/4 inch) in diameter and five to seven centimetres (two to 2-3/4 inches) deep.

Removing plugs of soil from the lawn allows water, oxygen and nutrients to reach the root zone. These holes cave in and loosen the soil under the grass. Aerating the lawn either in the spring or fall works just fine, providing that there is plenty of moisture in the soil.

Smaller lawns can be aerated using a manual aerator tool. These have two or four hollow cylinders that are plunged into the soil with your foot to remove plugs of soil. For larger lawns, it is more efficient to rent a power aerator with a coring attachment. Leave the plugs on the lawn and allow them to dry out. They will break up after the first mowing and act as light topdressing.

Make sure that the grass and soil are moist when using an aerator. Sandy soil does not benefit from aeration, since it already drains well and is less prone to compaction.

Using a manual aerator.

When using a broadcast fertilizer spreader, use 1/2 rate setting and go in a criss-cross pattern for even distribution.

SHOULD I FERTILIZE MY LAWN?

Throughout the growing season, a healthy lawn can grow over two metres (six feet) in total. To support this growth, your lawn needs a continuous supply of nutrition, particularly the three main nutrients: *nitrogen, phosphorus and potassium*.

Generally, nitrogen makes the lawn green, phosphorus produces healthy roots, and potassium builds hardiness while assisting in the effectiveness of the other two elements. Grass also needs calcium, magnesium and the other elements, but it can usually gather them unassisted from the soil, air and water.

Early in the spring, rake the lawn to remove any debris that has collected over the winter. Wait until the ground is dry enough to walk on without causing soil compaction (you will know when the time is right when you are able to walk on the lawn without leaving the impression of your shoe in it).

Fertilize with an organic based, slow-release nitrogen lawn food a purely organic fertilizer or spread finished compost about one to two centimetres (1/4 to 1/3 inch) thick. Use this opportunity to thicken your lawn with fresh grass seed (see below).

In early spring, rake debris out of your lawn, but don't work too hard at it or you risk damaging lawn roots.

Keep your lawn at least 2-1/2 inches long.

An enviro-friendly push mower.

MAINTAINING YOUR ORGANIC LAWN

MOWING

Keep the mower blades set high so the grass is always at least six centimetres (2 1/2 inches) high. This helps to keep weeds under control by crowding them out, and protects grass roots from drying out.

Longer grass has deeper roots. Don't scalp your lawn or try to imitate the look of your favourite golf course (unless you want the intense maintenance schedule of one!). If you want to rake the clippings, add them to the compost. Leave short clippings where they fall.

Better yet, use the mulching option on your power mower. This is ideal for large lawns as it chops the grass clippings and returns them to the soil where they break down and supply nutrients, especially nitrogen. For smaller lawns, a reel or push mower has an efficient, scissor-like cutting action that slices rather than tears the grass blades, giving a good clean cut.

Very quiet with no gas fumes or extension cords to worry about, reel mowers are the best option to reduce noise and air pollution in the neighbourhood.

Maintain mower blades twice a season to keep them sharp. Have you ever noticed a brown hue to either your lawn or your neighbour's? That is usually the result of using dull blades that tear not cut the grass. I sharpen my lawn mower blades twice a year.

It is not always necessary to mow the lawn every week. Mow it only when needed during the summer. You should never be removing more than 1/3 of the grass blade at a time.

A lawn is lush with lots of rain in spring, but to save water, let it go dormant in summer.

WATERING

Moisture is a key component in growing a thick, healthy lawn. During the early spring, there is usually enough rainfall to meet your lawn's needs, but once we hit late spring and early summer, heat arrives and with it the need to water once a week (never more). When you experience a drought (three weeks without rain), I recommend that you stop watering altogether.

Your lawn will go brown and dormant (and your water bill will hold steady or may even go down!) but the grass will bounce back when cool evening temperatures return and with them heavy morning dew and increased rainfall.

When you do water, it is best to water the lawn deeply and less frequently, which helps the grass plants develop a deep root system. Most healthy lawns require only 2.5 centimetres (one inch) of water each week. Many people overwater their lawn, sprinkling it lightly and often, which can lead to shallow roots and the ideal conditions for diseases and more weeds. Use a small plastic rain gauge or even an empty tuna can to measure lawn watering and avoid overwatering.

Hot and dry summer days cause the soil to lose a lot of moisture to evaporation, especially from about 11 a.m. through the afternoon. Water early in

A "heart breaker" sprinkler does the trick in the early morning.

the morning or in the evening to maximize the amount of water getting to the plant roots and minimize the amount of water lost to evaporation.

Your soil type will determine the rate at which you water the lawn. It is important not to water faster than the soil can absorb it. Stop watering when water starts to run off the lawn and on to the sidewalk or driveway. Clay soils retain water quite well, but sandy soils drain freely and can require more frequent watering.

KEY ELEMENT

TAKE CONTROL OF SPRINKLER SYSTEMS

Do you have an automatic, in-ground sprinkler system? Good. It can be very useful when used properly. To take full advantage of the benefits of your in-ground watering system, I recommend that you turn off the automatic feature of the system and turn on the manual function so you can control when the water is applied. Turn the system on for two to three hours once a week at most. During drought situations, do not water your lawn at all. Let it go dormant.

When mowing, do not cut the grass shorter than six to eight centimetres (2.5 to three inches), and avoid cutting more than one-third of the blade length to encourage deep root development and to reduce stress. Treat the lawn with organic garden sulfur if you notice moulds and fungus.

SHADE LAWNS

Growing a lawn in the shade can be challenging. Conditions can be improved by pruning the canopy of trees to allow more sunlight through. Select grass seed mixtures specifically developed for shade and be prepared to re-seed the area each year. Sheep fescues, red fescue, hard fescues, creeping fescue and chewings fescue (and their cultivars) are the most shade-tolerant grasses, although chewings fescue doesn't tolerate foot traffic and none of them spread quickly. They have narrow leaf blades and deep, fibrous root systems. Tall fescues, perennial ryegrass cultivars and a few cultivars of Kentucky bluegrass also have some shade tolerance.

A shade lawn is maintained differently than a lawn grown in full sun. Set your mower height higher (7.5 centimetres/three inches), and feed less. Too much nitrogen can be detrimental to shade grasses. Apply water deeply *once a week at most* and avoid heavy foot traffic.

Shade lawns are often susceptible to broadleaf weeds and moss, especially in maritime areas of the country. Moss can be discouraged by aerating the lawn (see "Should I aerate my lawn?" page 132) and by improving the site's drainage. Adding limestone to the soil is sometimes recommended to combat moss, but check your soil's pH before going this route.

If the pH is already high, adding limestone will not help and may very well hurt your lawn. (See Chapter 13 for more on pH.)

Sow lawn seed in mid-August through early fall for best results. Second best is an April/early May application of grass seed. Make sure that fallen leaves are promptly removed from the lawn so they don't mat and smother the lawn or impede growth of new grass.

Grass prefers alkaline soil.

A densely shaded yard is a difficult place to grow a lawn. Here, Lamium and hostas make cool substitutes.

LAWN SUBSTITUTES

If you have been caring for the lawn as described in this chapter and you continue to experience problems, there may simply be too little light for successful grass growing. Other perennial groundcovers might be more appropriate. Here are some of the better choices for a lawn substitute:

BUGLEWEED

(*Ajuga reptans*)
Zone 3. A low-growing plant with attractive foliage, it spreads via above-ground stolons and withstands light foot traffic. There are different cultivars available in different flower and foliage colours. It prefers moist, well-drained soils in heavy shade to full sun.

LILY OF THE VALLEY

(*Convallaria majalis*)
Zone 2. Spreading rapidly via rhizomes, it forms a thick carpet of upright leaves, with fragrant white flowers in mid-spring. It may go dormant in summer, and will not withstand foot traffic. Incredibly hardy, it adapts to many conditions but does best in well-drained soils in partial to full shade.

PURPLELEAF WINTERCREEPER

(*Euonymus fortunei* 'Coloratus')
Zone 3. Forming a dense carpet of dark green leaves, this perennial groundcover has a trailing habit which allows plants to root easily into the soil as they spread. It won't withstand foot traffic. Growing well in full shade to full sun, it prefers well-drained soils.

COMMON PERIWINKLE

(*Vinca minor*)
Zone 3. A very popular evergreen groundcover, periwinkle forms a dense mat of glossy dark green leaves with bright blue flowers in spring. It grows in fairly heavy shade and has a trailing habit with stems that easily root along the ground. It withstands moderate foot traffic. Mow the patch after blooming every couple of years to keep it thick and keep down weeds. Also watch it doesn't escape from the garden as it can become an invasive pest in the wild.

Periwinkle (Vinca minor).

JAPANESE SPURGE

(*Pachysandra terminalis*)
Zone 3. A handsome evergreen groundcover with a neat and uniform growth habit, Japanese spurge spreads via rhizomes to form a thick carpet. Plants bear clusters of white flowers in spring. It tolerates poor soil but prefers well-drained loam, and will not tolerate foot traffic.

VIRGINIA CREEPER

(*Parthenocissus quinquefolia*)
Zone 4. This hardy, vigorous grower has root-like tendrils that attach themselves to any textured surface. It will grow in any fertile, well-drained soil in shade or sun. This plant can wreak havoc in your garden if planted in the wrong place. Only plant it where you can keep it in check. Prune back to the main stems in spring to keep it under control.

In one handful of quality garden soil there are many billions of microorganisms.

CHAPTER THIRTEEN
The Beauty of Soil

I heard recently that we actually know less about what goes on under the surface of the soil than we do about what goes on at the bottom of the ocean. Whether this is true or not, one thing I do know is that well-fed soil produces the best-looking plants.

Quote me any time:

90 percent of success in your garden is the direct result of proper soil preparation.

Gorgeous, late-season blooming rose of Sharon.

While certain types of soil will make gardening easier or more challenging, understanding the type of soil you have and its strengths and weaknesses will help you determine what you can grow in it.

SOIL COMPOSITION

Healthy, fertile soil will not only lead to vibrant blooms, verdant foliage and abundant fruits and vegetables but also eliminate the need for pesticides and synthetic fertilizers. If you are a keen organic gardener, soil improvement is the essential first step, and maintenance is an important follow-up.

Good garden soil is composed of minerals (45 per cent), air (25 per cent), water (25 per cent), and organic matter (5 per cent).

MINERALS

The bulk of the soil, the mineral portion, is made up of tiny rock particles that not only provide some of the mineral nutrients that plants need but also largely determine the soil's texture. The particles vary in size, the very smallest being those that make clay, the next in size being silt, and the largest being sand.

The amount of each size particle in the soil determines how well that particular soil drains and holds water (and nutrients) and how much air it contains. Sand is coarse, and because the spaces between particles (called pore spaces) are big, the particles do not stick together or compact. Sand therefore cannot hold water or nutrients well; they tend to flow through sand quickly.

Sand will, however, warm up faster in the spring and, when present in the soil by no more than 40 percent, is a useful ingredient in any good-quality garden soil. Clay particles do hold nutrients well because there are more pore spaces and more particle surface for water to cling to, but they tend to stick together and can be compacted. Severe compaction creates "hardpan," which is extremely dense, hard soil.

Mixtures of clay, silt and sand are called "loams." The ideal loam is roughly 40 percent sand, 40 percent silt and 20 percent clay. My dad always swore by sandy loam, which has a higher ratio of sand, as the best possible start to a garden. It is easy to dig and easy for plants to root in. A good loam has pore space that accounts for between 30 and 50 per cent of the volume of the soil, allowing water and oxygen to circulate freely.

AIR

We don't often think of soil as being composed of air but, indeed, when you have good soil, a quarter of its volume will be air (the three primary components of which are, of course, nitrogen, oxygen and carbon dioxide). The soil microorganisms that keep the cycle of decomposition moving (and manufacture many of the nutrients on which our plants rely) need oxygen to survive.

Nitrogen in gas form is also essential so that bacteria can consume it and turn it into a water-soluble form that plants can absorb. What's more, roots need to breathe and depend on good air exchange between soil and atmosphere.

WATER

The necessity for water in soil is obvious to any gardener. Water not only carries nutrients from the soil to the roots in a form that the roots can absorb, but also maintains the plant's cell structure. But the mere presence of water in the soil is not enough. Sandy soils don't retain water well and plants may go thirsty without vigilant watering; on the other hand, clay soils can hold water too well. Water and clay bond together strongly (not unlike a magnetic attraction), so the plant roots may not be able to remove the water molecules from the clay bond, and the plant will remain parched. In addition, with this tight bond between water and clay, pore spaces are filled with water, squeezing out necessary air.

Organic matter eventually breaks down to form humus.

WHAT IS HUMUS?

The terms humus and compost are often used interchangeably, but humus is actually organic matter in the very final stages of decomposition, while compost is material that is largely decomposed, but may contain identifiable bits of matter—eggshell, leaves or twigs, etc. Compost is rich in humus, as is leaf mould. Nutrient-rich, humus has a soft, sticky texture and contributes greatly to the friability of the soil.

ORGANIC MATTER

Organic matter is the smallest component of soil, yet the one that can have the greatest effect on how the other three interact and how well your plants do. Organic material or humus is found in finished compost. Humus is the decayed remains of organic or once-living material—in other words, decomposed plant and animal material. Humus provides food for microorganisms, bacteria, fungi, insects and earthworms that convert the nutrients it contains into soluble forms that plant roots can absorb.

It can also contribute macronutrients (nutrients that plants need in large quantities) such as nitrogen, phosphorus and potassium, as well as micronutrients or trace elements (nutrients plants need in small quantities) directly to the soil.

Organic material such as compost and leaf mould (partly decomposed leaves) also affects the structure of the soil. It makes clay more workable or friable (meaning it will crumble more easily). And by increasing pore space, it also improves air and water circulation (sometimes referred to as improving a soil's *tilth*). In sandy soils, it allows the soil to retain more moisture and nutrients.

Okay, are you asleep yet? This subject may not equal the latest computer game in terms of edge-of-the-seat entertainment, but understanding what makes good soil is the most important knowledge a gardener can have. Just as you learned what you should eat to maintain a healthy diet, you need to know what to feed the soil to have a healthy garden.

Encourage earthworms, the foot soldiers of the garden!

KEY ELEMENT

THE WORM TEST

The best soil test that you can do as an organic gardener is what I call the "worm test." All it takes is a spade or a shovel.

Dig a hole about 30 centimetres (12 inches) deep. Turn over the soil that you have removed from the hole and break it up (hit it with the back of the shovel if you need to). Now bend down and look for worms. See any? The more the better.

If you don't find any worms at first, don't give up. Keep digging and searching. After you have a pretty good idea of the quantity of worms at work in your garden, consider enhancing the population by adding compost to your garden soil. I add at least two centimetres (just under an inch) each year in spring or fall ---it doesn't matter--- to my entire garden.

The goal is to grow your earthworm population; do the worm test on your soil each year and you'll soon learn if you are on the right track. Apart from the performance of your garden plants, this test will become one of the tests of your success as a gardener.

DETERMINING YOUR SOIL TYPE

If you have been digging in your garden, you no doubt know if you are dealing with very sandy soil or very heavy clay. But if you have been fortunate enough to escape the extremes, you may want to try one of the following simple tests to see where your soil composition lies on the spectrum.

1. JAR TEST

Take 250 millilitres (one cup) of garden soil and place it in a one-litre (four-cup) jar. Fill the rest of the jar with tap water and shake until the soil and water are mixed. Let the jar rest undisturbed for at least 24 hours. You will begin to see the soil settle.

When the water at the top is almost clear, you should see that the soil has separated into layers. Sand will settle at the bottom. The next layer will be silt, followed by clay on top. The organic matter will float in and on top of the

The soil "jar test" is simple and fun.

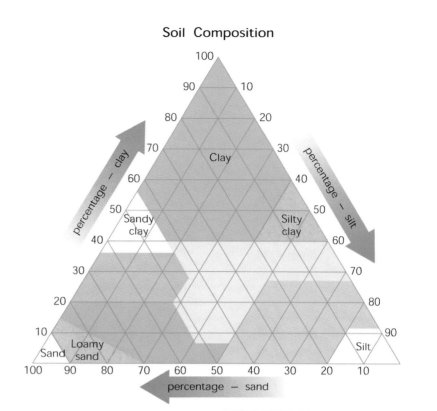

Soil Composition

water. Check the ratio of sand, silt and clay against the diagram above to determine what kind of soil you have.

2. HAND TEST

You can also determine your soil type by appearance and feel. Clay soil is generally yellowish-tan in colour; loam is usually light to dark brown; and sandy soil tends to be greyish-tan. To identify your soil type by feel, try this test two or three days after it has rained. Pick up a small quantity of soil (about the size of a golf ball). Squeeze it between thumb and index finger, or close your hand around it, and then let go.

If it feels gritty and falls apart as soon as you release it, it contains a high proportion of sand. If it feels smooth and silky, but holds its shape for a short time before it crumbles into chunks, it is loam. If it feels like moist talcum powder (some people say it feels "greasy"), it is high in silt. If it is slippery or sticky, and holds its shape even after you have released it, it is mostly clay

1. Pick up a small amount of moist soil.

2. Close hand around soil.

3. Release the soil and see how much it crumbles.

Blueberries require acidic soil with a low pH.

UNDERSTANDING SOIL pH

When it comes to soil and soil improvement, it is a good idea to spend some time determining the chemical nature of your soil as well as its physical composition. This means understanding pH—not always an easy thing to do. The pH scale measures the concentration of hydrogen ions in a substance. This concentration determines the relative acidity or alkalinity of a substance, in this case, your soil. The pH of your soil can affect not only what plants thrive and which suffer in your garden, but how nutritious your soil is for your plants.

The most acidic end of the pH scale is 1. Concentrated hydrochloric acid, for example, would be around 1, and white vinegar around 3. The extreme alkaline end of the pH scale is 14 (household ammonia ranks about 11). Seven is the midpoint of the scale, indicating neutrality.

Most plants grow best in soil with a close-to-neutral pH of 6 to 7. Anything below 4.5 or above 8 is generally inhospitable for plants. Although pH itself is no indication of the nutrient content of soil, the level of pH affects the availability of soil nutrients to plants. Helpful microorganisms including nitrogen-fixing bacteria and mycorrhizae cannot live in highly acidic soil. Conversely, plants cannot take up iron in very alkaline soil, even though the soil itself might be quite rich with the mineral. This is a problem for plants such as rhododendrons that need unusually high quantities of iron.

These acid-loving plants—rhodos, as well as ferns, azaleas, camellias and blueberries—like an acidic soil with a pH between 4.5 and 5.5. For plants such as asparagus, spinach and cacti that prefer a mildly alkaline soil, we are talking about soil in the 7.5 pH range. Those number ranges might sound rather slight, but the pH scale is logarithmic, like the Richter scale for measuring earthquakes. Each number indicates a value 10 times the previous number, so a soil with a pH of 9 is 10 times more alkaline than a soil with a pH of 8, and 100 times more alkaline than a soil of pH 7!

It's a good idea to grow plants that like your soil's existing pH. Amending soil to change it is an uphill battle. Adding lime to raise the pH, for example, or digging in sulfur to lower the pH will generally change the soil chemistry for only one growing season before the soil reverts to its natural pH. This means you will have to amend on an annual or semi-annual basis. Organic material, however, will moderate pH for longer than the synthetic alternatives. Humus keeps soil in the neutral range and helps plants to thrive in soil outside their pH comfort zone.

Weeds such as dandelions are indicators of soil pH.

You can make a rough estimate of the pH of your soil by assessing the wild plant life that grows on your property or in your neighbourhood. Sorrel or horsetail weeds, dandelion, plantain, knotweed, mosses, nettles, oxeye daisy, ferns, blueberries, rhododendrons and trees such as hemlock, red spruce, oak and white pine all thrive in acidic soil. Campion, stinkweed and nodding thistle, pinks, evening primrose, Eastern white cedar, ash, barberry and lilac prefer alkaline soil.

HOW TO TEST FOR pH

Many experienced gardeners will advise you to test your soil for pH regularly or at least as often as you encounter unexplained plant problems. The easiest way to do this is to use a home soil testing kit, available at most garden centres or hardware stores. Remember, when performing any sort of home pH test, you must use distilled water.

An inexpensive soil test kit is easy to use.

You can also purchase portable pH meters, although they can be quite expensive, or send soil samples for professional testing that will include a pH test.

Simple litmus paper can also give you quite reliable results and is a good deal cheaper. To use litmus paper, add dis-tilled water to a small quantity of soil until you have a thick liquid consistency. Let this mud stand for an hour (adding water if it dries out). Then dip the strip of litmus paper in the mud and leave it for a minute. Rinse the strip with distilled water and match the colour of the paper to the pH chart that comes with the paper.

Remember that soil can vary from spot to spot in your garden so test a number of areas, especially if you have a large garden. You may find slightly more alkaline conditions next to your house, where calcium can leach from the concrete foundation.

GARDEN BEDS FOR SPECIALIZED PLANTS

Some gardeners decide to create a sep-arate bed for plants that like soil conditions not found elsewhere in their garden. If they have neutral or slightly alkaline soils, for example, they may create an "acid bed" where they can plant rhododendrons or azaleas. Amending one moderately sized bed is a far easier task than trying to convert an entire garden, and you may find that if you are working on only one spot, you won't mind the continual upkeep. To create an acid bed, you might dump your coffee grounds straight onto the soil instead of in the composter, grind and add your citrus fruit rinds to the soil or work in fallen pine needles. In other words, a continual variety of small acts will reinforce the acidity.

Lilacs prefer an alkaline soil with a high pH.

PLANTS FOR ACID SOIL

ACID-LOVERS (optimum pH: 5 to 6)
Bleeding heart (*Dicentra formosa*)
Blueberries (*Vaccinium corymbosum*)
English daisy (*Bellis perennis*)
Goldenrod (*Solidago*)
Heathers (*Erica* spp.)
Japanese andromeda (*Pieris japonica*)
Lily (*Lilium*)
Lily of the valley (*Convallaria*)
Magnolia (*Magnolia*)
Maidenhair fern (*Adiantum pedatum*)
Rhododendrons and azaleas (*Rhododendron* spp.)
Serviceberry (*Amelanchier canadensis*)
Veronica (*Veronica*)
Wild ginger (*Asarum canadense*)

VEGETABLES (pH 5.5 to 7)
Artichoke
Carrots
Corn
Eggplant (to 6.5 pH only)
Potatoes (to 6.5 pH only)
Sweet Potatoes (to 6 pH only)
Turnips and rutabagas

PLANTS FOR ALKALINE SOIL

ALKALINE-LOVERS
Asparagus (6 to 8)
Baby's breath (*Gypsophila paniculata*) (7 to 7.5)
Canna (*Canna*) (6 to 8)
Cotoneaster (*Cotoneaster*) (6 to 8)
Crocus (*Crocus*) (6 to 8)
Delphiniums (*Delphinium elatum*) (6 to 8)
Forget-me-not (*Myosotis*) (6 to 8)
Forsythia (*Forsythia*) (6 to 8)
Hepatica (*Hepatica*) (6 to 8)
Honeysuckle (*Lonicera*) (6 to 8)
Lilacs (*Syringa* spp.) (6 to 7.5)
Pasque flower (*Pulsatilla vulgaris*)
Peonies (*Paeonia lactiflora*) (6 to 7.5)
Phlox (*Phlox*) (6 to 8)
Poppy (*Papaver*) (6 to 8)
Sweet William (*Dianthus barbatus*) (6 to 7.5)

Bleeding heart.

Goldenrod.

Carrots.

▼ *Poppies.* ▲ *Lilac.*

For triple mix, combine quality topsoil with equal parts peat and compost.

SOIL WARNING

Only buy topsoil from a reputable company or by the bag from a retailer you trust. Very often, "topsoil for sale" classified ads in the newspaper are put in by people who are clearing land for development and who are not in the soil business. What they consider "good" topsoil may be no better than the stuff you are already struggling with in your garden! Triple mix—an equal mix of topsoil, peat moss and compost—may be more expensive if you are replacing a large area, but it has the advantage of already containing soil amendments and conditioners. Again, use a supplier that you trust.

SOIL FERTILITY - UNDERSTANDING NPK

While the physical composition of the soil will affect aeration, water percolation and the ease with which you can work the stuff, the fertility of the soil is essential in determining how healthy your plants will be. Plants' primary need is for nitrogen (N), phosphorus (P) and potassium (K). These macronutrients are always listed in the same order in descriptions or on packaging, indicating the percentage of each nutrient that the material contains. For example, a box of bone meal might have the numbers 2-14-0 indicating that, of the total contents, it has two percent nitrogen, 14 percent phosphorus and 0 percent potassium.

Plants also need magnesium, calcium and sulfur (often referred to as secondary nutrients). As well as these

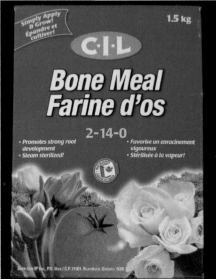

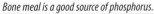

Bone meal is a good source of phosphorus.

macronutrients, plants need many other elements in much smaller quantities (micronutrients), such as iron, manganese, zinc, chlorine, boron, copper and nickel. These nutrients are consumed by the plants, so some of the elements (mainly the macronutrients) need to be replaced in the soil on a continual basis. Decomposing organic material does just this by slowly releasing the elements over a long period of time into the soil.

There are many natural sources of the elements that your plants need the most —blood meal features nitrogen (12-0-0), bone meal has phosphorus (2-14-0), blood and bone meal provides a balance of both (7-7-0) and muriate of potash, also known as potassium chloride, provides potassium (0-0-60).

REPLACING AND AMENDING SOIL

Soil improvement may be a long process, especially if you are starting with very poor soil (think two to four years), but all soil benefits from a yearly or bi-yearly application of organic matter; otherwise, your soil will become less fertile over time. I recommend that you add no less than two to four centimetres (3/4 to 1 1/2 inches) of new organic material—finished compost, well-rotted cattle manure, mushroom compost or composted leaves— to your beds each year, in either spring or fall. You'll need 40 kilos (90 pounds) of compost to cover 10 square metres (100 square feet).

Some gardeners insist that the compost must be dug into the soil, but of course this poses a problem when you've got established perennial beds, especially if they are closely planted. I simply lay the compost on top of the beds in April or May before too much has come up. By July, earthworms and other soil organisms have pulled the organic matter down into the soil, doing all the work for me. Their action also causes the beds to settle, so even yearly applications won't raise the beds unduly.

If, however, you are establishing new beds or planting new plants, by all means work in compost, manure and other soil amendments well.

If your soil is very poor or unsuitable for the plants you have your heart set on, I recommend that you dig out the existing garden beds, remove the existing soil and order high-quality sandy loam or triple mix to replace it.

If your soil is so hard and clay-like that you need a pickaxe to dig it, you will need to remove it to a depth of at least 45 centimetres (18 inches) for annuals and perennials and 60 centimetres (two feet) for evergreens, shrubs and roses. Make sure that the new soil is 10 centimetres (four inches) above grade because the bed will settle by about 20 percent in the first year. Also, organic microbial activity in the soil will cause it to settle further each year (which is why you should top it up with finished compost every year).

I look happy because I am. What a good cook sees in raw veggies (a fine meal), I see in this compost pile (a fabulous garden).

GOING ORGANIC

Organic fertilizers and amendments improve soil structure as well as add fertility to the soil. The decomposing organic material aerates and conditions the soil, making it friable, as the microorganisms work their way through. And of course organic material attracts the insects and microorganisms in the first place. Indeed, organic gardeners believe in feeding the soil before the plants, for all these reasons.

If you are adding plenty of organic material, like compost or composted manure, to your soil each year, you generally do not need to worry about further feeding your garden. But some plants, like vegetables, are fast growing and therefore need and absorb a great deal of these nutrients from the soil. You may need to feed your vegetable beds regularly with compost tea (compost steeped in water overnight, usually in a burlap sack, to create a liquid that contains the nutrients that are now dissolved in the water).

WHY NOT USE SYNTHETIC OR CHEMICAL FERTILIZER?

Synthetic fertilizers add the elements directly to the soil for consumption by the plants but lack the complexities of all-natural fertilizers. It is the complexities of organic amendments that help to feed and support the soil. Remember the mantra of the organic gardener: feed the soil and the plants will take care of themselves.

That said, the use of synthetic fertilizers exclusively over a period of time will rob your soil of its natural organic ingredients. You will end up with "hungry soil," which is not well suited to supporting plant life.

Wondering if a fertilizer is organic or synthetic? Most often the label will tell you everything that you need to know. However, if the total percentage of nitrogen, phosphorus and potassium equals more than 15, you can be pretty sure that it is not all organic.

The excessive use of synthetic fertilizers causes soil quality to deteriorate, leaving the soil compacted and dense, with little air circulation (leading to plants and microorganisms being starved of air); in sandy soil, synthetic fertilizers do nothing to add water retention and may, in fact, not get to the plant at all as they leach through the soil quickly when it rains. This leaching of synthetic fertilizers can pollute groundwater.

KEY ELEMENT

WHEN IS COMPOSTING LIKE SEX?
According to www.grist.org, composting has a lot in common with sex... it's a healthy, natural process involving fertility, tumbling around, and... when it is going right—steaminess. On top of that, some people call it dirty.

Courtesy the Ontario Ministry of the Environment (and you wonder what they do all day?)

ORGANIC SOIL AMENDMENTS

Even organic soil additions should be applied with care. It's important to understand what you are adding and why. Have a soil test done (see page 150) and determine what elements might be lacking in your soil before adding amendments willy-nilly.

BLOOD MEAL
- A good source of nitrogen
- Releases nutrients slowly
- Add to soil when planting bulbs to deter squirrels
- Apply 4.5 to 13.5 kilos per 93 square metres (10 to 30 pounds per 1,000 square feet) depending on soil fertility

Blood meal.

BONE MEAL
- A good source of phosphorus and calcium
- Releases nutrients slowly
- Apply 4.5 to 13.5 kilos per 93 square metres (10 to 30 pounds per 1,000 square feet) depending on soil fertility
- Has little effect on pH

Bone Meal

CITRUS RINDS
- Ground-up rinds worked into soil will lower pH slightly, that is, make soil more acidic.

COFFEE GROUNDS
- A source of nitrogen
- A good addition to compost, but can be dug into the soil as well
- Will lower pH slightly (make soil more acidic)
- Tea leaves and teabags have similar properties

COMPOST
- An excellent source of organic matter
- Contains trace elements such as zinc, copper, manganese
- Is naturally slow release (apply spring and fall)
- Attracts earthworms and other beneficial insects and microorganisms
- Improves drainage and air circulation in clay soils
- Improves water retention, texture and volume of sandy soils
- Creates soil with a darker colour that absorbs heat faster in the spring and gives plants a quicker start
- Helps keep soil pH neutral
- Use backyard composters to produce your own or see if compost is available from a municipal large-scale leaf composting service. Good quality, well-rotted manure is a fine substitute.

COIR
- Provides excellent water retention
- Adds organic matter and lasts up to 3 times longer in the soil than peat moss
- Is all natural and renewable (come from the fibre of the coconut)
- Is high in salts and therefore must be worked thoroughly into the soil
- ph 5.5 to 6.0

A coir brick, before adding water.

EGGSHELLS
- Provide calcium and some trace minerals
- Can be added to composter or soil
- May deter slugs when placed around plants
- Useful when planting tomatoes to deter blossom-end rot (add eggshells from two eggs per plant)

Leaves left to rot all winter become "leaf mould" by mid- to late spring.

LEAF MOULD
- A good source of humus and therefore nutrients
- Improves soil structure
- Decomposes rapidly so is not a long-lasting source of nutrients

FEATHER MEAL
- Ground feathers from poultry
- A slow-release source of nitrogen
- Apply 4.5 to 13.5 kilos per 93 square metres (10 to 30 pounds per 1,000 square feet) depending on soil fertility

ORGANIC GRANULAR COMMERCIAL FERTILIZER
Read label to be sure that the product is from organic sources.
- Generally derived from fish meal, rock phosphate, greensand, gypsum and kelp meal
- See package information for NPK and remember that organic fertilizers generally total less than 15 when you add up all 3 numbers.
- Slow release
- Apply to soil as required
- May contain trace elements
- Does not improve soil structure

ORGANIC LIQUID COMMERCIAL FERTILIZER
Read the label to be sure that the product is organic. Sea kelp, compost tea and fish fertilizer are popular examples of liquid fertilizer.
- Can be applied to foliage—plants readily absorb nutrients through leaf pores
- Quicker release than granular; use once a month or every two weeks
- See package information for NPK
- Usually contains trace elements
- Does not improve soil structure

FISH EMULSION
- Made from fish by-products dissolved in water
- A good source of nitrogen
- Contains trace elements
- Can be applied in liquid form to foliage
- Doesn't smell as bad as you might think if used outdoors

GROUND BARK OR SAWDUST
- Adds texture and volume to sandy soil; not recommended for clay soil
- Decomposes slowly

- Can rob the soil of nitrogen so add it with a nitrogen-rich fertilizer
- Sawdust should be well rotted before use
- Apply sawdust 4.5 to 13.5 kilos per 93 square metres (10 to 30 pounds per 1,000 square feet) depending on soil composition
- Fertilizer value is negligible

COMPOST OR MANURE TEA
- Contains small quantities of macro- (primarily nitrogen) and micronutrients
- Can be used frequently as a nutrient booster
- Can be applied to soil or foliage

WELL-ROTTED ANIMAL MANURE
(cattle, steer, horse, sheep, chicken or other herbivores)
- A naturally slow-release source of nutrients
- **SHEEP MANURE** (dry) - NPK: 4-1.4-3.5. Apply 11 to 45 kilos per 93 square metres (25 to 100 pounds per 1,000 square feet)
- **COW MANURE** (dry) - NPK: 2-2.3-2.4. Apply 45 to 90 kilos per 93 square metres (100 to 200 pounds per 1,000 square feet)
- **HORSE MANURE** - NPK: 1.7-0.7-1.8. Apply 45 to 90 kilos per 93 square metres (100 to 200 pounds per 1,000 square feet) Must be composted as fresh manure will burn plants. Raw manure can be added to your compost pile to break down with the other material
- Loosens clay soils and improves drainage
- Improves the texture of sandy soils

MUSHROOM COMPOST (MY FAVOURITE COMPOST!)
- Same benefits as compost, but it will make soil more alkaline (this can be offset by adding sulfur)
- Weed-free
- Mix with equal parts sandy loam to create the perfect general-purpose garden soil

My first mentor in the gardening business, Kees Moorlag, would say, "The difference between sheep and cattle manure is how far it falls." Experience has since taught me that he was right—as far as the plants are concerned.

PEAT MOSS

- Has a pH of 3.0 to 4.5, so lowers pH (increases acidity)
- Improves water retention in sandy soil (can hold up to 20 times its weight in water)
- Improves water and air circulation in sandy and clay soils
- Must be wetted through before being dug well into soil

Peat moss.

WOOD ASH

- A good source of potassium (potash) and calcium
- Will raise pH (make soil alkaline); twice as strong as lime
- Must be from plain untreated wood or paper
- Mixed with water, it creates lye, which is caustic, so mix ashes with other soil amendments (except fresh manure) before adding to soil; don't let it touch plants
- Sprinkled on the earth around plants, it repels slugs, cutworms, snails, root aphids, vine borers and other pests. Make a depression around a plant and fill with a little ash
- Can be "leached" of lye by running water through it
- Should be free of nails, screws, staples, etc. if coming from your fireplace

WORM CASTINGS

- A good source of nutrients and microorganisms
- Contain 50 per cent organic matter and 11 trace minerals
- Improves water retention
- Can be purchased or made at home by using worms to compost your kitchen waste

INORGANIC AMENDMENTS

CLAY

- Add to sandy soils along with organic material to improve water retention

EPSOM SALTS

- Source of magnesium (10%) and sulfur (13%)—some rose growers swear by it for enhancing rose growth
- Apply 0.5 to 2.2 kilos per 93 square metres (one to five pounds per 1,000 square feet)

HORTICULTURAL GYPSUM

- Is calcium sulfate so good source of calcium (22%) and sulfur (17%).
- Helps correct excess magnesium or sodium content of soil
- Loosens clay soil
- Does not affect soil pH
- Do not apply if pH is below 5.8

DOLOMITIC LIMESTONE

- Finely ground limestone
- Raises soil pH
- A source of calcium (51% calcium carbonate) and magnesium (40% magnesium carbonate)

SHARP OR COARSE SAND

- Added to clay soils to improve air circulation and drainage
- Use with other organic amendments for fertility
- Avoid sandbox sand, which is too fine and smooth and will compact

Dolomitic limestone.

Sharp sand.

SULFUR

- Lowers pH (makes soil more acidic)
- To lower pH one unit, apply 4.5 kilos per 93 square metres (10 pounds per 1,000 square feet), depending on soil composition
- Overuse can damage plants and disrupt the chemical balance of the soil
- May be ineffective on strongly alkaline soils

VERMICULITE

- Shiny, porous flakes of superheated mica (a natural element)
- Can be used in sandy soil to improve air circulation and water and nutrient retention
- Larger granular size than perlite
- Less expensive than perlite, but does not last as long
- Is not dusty like perlite
- Contains small amounts of potassium and magnesium
- pH 7 to 7.5

Vermiculite.

PROFESSIONAL SOIL TESTING

As mentioned earlier, professional soil testing is available through various soil-testing services across the country as well as many full-service garden centres. Labs will screen the soil for pH, macronutrients and organic matter, and can test for specific micronutrients or other chemicals and elements at your request (generally, the labs have an agronomist who will speak with you about your specific concerns and can help you determine what other things should be tested for). The basic tests are usually relatively inexpensive, but all other specific screens can be quite costly. A professional test should come with a summary that tells you how you should treat the soil to remedy any deficiencies.

But do you need a professional soil test? If your home test indicates deficiencies or problems that you might need to address with the addition of lime, rock phosphate, greensand, gypsum, sulfur or Epsom salts, you may very well want to reconfirm these results with a professional test before adding any of these sorts of ingredients. Too much of any of them may cause other problems, and you will need to know quite specifically how much is demanded.

You may also want to have a professional test done if you have a history of plants performing poorly in an area even though they have been given appropriate care. Testing is a wise investment if you are putting in a vegetable garden, as vegetables demand adequate levels of nutrients to flourish.

Consider getting a test done if you have concerns about contamination on your property (whether from a nearby industry or previous use of the land). You will have to know what chemicals or elements you are looking for, however, and the lab may be able to help you there. Keep in mind that if the land your home was recently built on was previously the home of any industry, the developer may have had to have the soil tested and approved, and these documents should be available for you.

PREPARING SOIL SAMPLES FOR A PROFESSIONAL TEST

If you decide to get a professional test done, make sure that you get accurate results by preparing your samples properly. Use only plastic or stainless steel tools (other metals may leave traces of metals or minerals that will alter your soil sample). Dig a small hole to a depth of 15 centimetres (six inches) for beds or 10 cm (four inches) for soil under lawns and then take a slice all the way down the side of this hole. Make sure that the sample is free of mulch or other debris from the surface.

As with home testing, you may want to have a number of areas of your yard tested, but this will be more expensive. If you wish to do a follow-up each year to see if your amendments are improving the soil, make sure to take samples at the same time each year (soil content can vary throughout the season). And keep in mind that fall is usually a less busy time for testing labs, so you may get your results faster then.

A fabulous field of sunflowers growing in very good soil, you can be sure. Photo taken by Larry Parr at the Eden project in Devon, England.

Now, if you have successfully read through this whole chapter, it will perhaps come as a surprise that building a healthy soil is the most exciting part of gardening, from my point of view.

While you may think that I am nuts, let me assure you that I am not alone. Just you wait—as you learn the pros and cons of building better soil, you will also experience the thrill of the results. Ahhhhhh! Like most anything else, the results provide us with

the acid (sorry for the pun) test! Try feeding your soil and, and eventually (maybe three years from now), you will see what I mean. Believe me, the process will become addictive—and you'll wonder why you didn't do it sooner.

An enviable collection of well-used hand tools—the stories they could tell! —at the Lost Gardens of Heligan, Cornwall, England.

CHAPTER FOURTEEN
Planting for Success

For me, planting is the highlight of gardening tasks. I think of putting plants into the ground as an artist thinks of their paints—using plants we create pictures that live. And because they live, they are ever changing, which makes gardening a rare art form indeed as it is always a work in progress.

Apart from the sheer joy of working good rich soil, your goal when planting is to get seeds, bulbs, young plants

Garden digging fork.

Cultivator.

Traditional garden shovel.

and transplants into the ground, while ensuring to the greatest extent possible that they grow where they are planted.

D-handled shovel.

To achieve this, spend some time before you plant—in fact, before you even choose your plants—deciding where they will go. Keep in mind the mature size of the plants, both height and spread, and their individual needs for sunlight, moisture and soil nutrients. Avoid putting plants in a spot they will quickly outgrow and keep in mind that trees and shrubs can create havoc with their roots if they are planted too close to walls and paved areas.

"The right plant in the right place will not only ensure the plant's success but will also save you labour and heartache."

THE IMPORTANCE OF DIGGING

In planting just like painting, preparation is key. Of course, you must have good soil (see Chapter 13) and the planting area must be readied, which usually means digging. For most people, digging is digging, right? Well, yes and no. Like cookbooks, gardening books often use a number of terms to refer to different techniques.

FORKING is a method of loosening soil by pushing a garden fork into the earth and twisting it. (There are a number of fork substitutes on the market that make the lifting and twisting motion slightly easier.)

This helps to aerate the soil and improve drainage. It also improves soil that has been compacted by heavy rains or foot traffic, and loosens the roots of shallow weeds so they can be removed.

DIGGING generally refers to removing soil to the depth of your spade and turning it over on the spot or removing it altogether.

After single digging , your back may hurt, but your soul will feel revived.

Single and double-digging are ways to prepare beds, small and large, for planting. The techniques are similar, although double-digging involves going down much deeper and, often, loosening the subsoil. Single-dig your beds if you are preparing a site that has not been used for gardening before or for several years. Double-dig your bed if the drainage is bad or if your soil is poor and needs a great deal of amending and improving before planting. This deep digging is especially beneficial to root crops such as carrots and beets, which need the open soil and likely the addition of sand to lighten their journey down through the earth.

SINGLE-DIGGING A BED

Mark the area to be dug and divide it into sections about 30 centimetres (one foot) wide (their length will depend on the size of the bed you are digging). Dig down about 25 cm (10 inches) along the first section, creating a trench, and place this soil in a wheelbarrow or on a tarp.

Starting in the adjacent section, dig down again, this time moving the soil into the empty trench. This is your opportunity to enrich the soil with quantities of compost or composted manure—layering it in the bottom of the trench before refilling and/or mixing it with the soil as you dig.

Continue to dig the consecutive sections this way until you reach the last trench. Fill this last trench with the soil removed from the first one you dug. Always remove weeds, stones and other debris from the soil as you dig it.

DOUBLE-DIGGING A BED

Double-digging uses the same method of moving soil from one trench into the previously dug trench, but the digging is deeper and more compost is added. With this method, you may either dig down a full 60 centimetres (two feet) or dig out 30 centimetres (one foot) of soil and simply loosen the next 30 centimetres (one foot) at the bottom of the trench with a fork.

Either way, you should spread a layer of compost or well-rotted manure along the bottom of each empty trench before filling it with soil. Mix more compost with the soil as you add it or cover the entire bed with another layer of organic material once you've finished the bed. Double-digging is real work but you should only have to do it once and the benefits are immense.

Late-season ornamental millet and orange canna lilies make a dramatic combination.

Ornamental grasses are best planted in spring, as they thrive in the hotter, drier weather of summer. If you plant ornamental grasses in the autumn, be sure to plant in well-drained soil to minimize possible root rot.

Magnolias are best planted in spring.

SPRING OR FALL PLANTING?

Optimum planting times are spring and fall. Annual bedding plants—as well as summer-flowering bulbs such as dahlias and cannas—are planted in the spring for summer and early fall bloom. Most gardeners also do all their perennial planting in the spring. I can understand this—the garden centres are bursting with new plant stock, the days are tantalizingly long and gardeners have itchy fingers after months in winter gloves.

Bare-root plants (many roses, shrubs and trees, for example) should be planted in early spring while they are still dormant. And trees that have fleshy roots or are slow to establish—magnolia, dogwood, tulip tree, sweet-gum, red maple, birch, hawthorn, poplar, cherry, plum, crabapple and many oaks—are best saved for spring planting. But my experience has taught me that many trees, shrubs and perennials, especially peonies and irises, perform better when planted in fall. The cool, moist days of autumn prevent soil and plant dehydration, and the soil stays warm long enough to allow roots to develop before the onset of winter. This gives the plants a strong, early start on growth the following spring.

Most garden centres provide excellent discounts in the fall as they reduce inventory—a good thing for the thrifty gardener.

Plant tulips in the fall.

Rose of Sharon seedlings ready to be hardened off.

Fall is the time to plant spring-flowering bulbs such as tulips, daffodils, crocuses, etc. It is also a fine option if you grow your own seedlings of winter-hardy plant material like some herbs and many perennials. These can be started in a protective area over the summer (plant seeds in midsummer) and then transferred to their permanent homes in the fall. If you buy young plants from a nursery for fall planting, make sure they are in good shape —not leggy, root-bound, diseased or dehydrated— before you purchase them.

Always apply a winter mulch of fallen leaves at least 15 centimetres (six inches) thick, or five to six centimetres (two to 2 1/2 inches) of finely ground-up bark to newly planted fall beds to prevent the plants from heaving out of the ground during freeze-thaw cycles.

PLANTING SEEDS

When sowing seeds, always make sure that the soil is well prepared, as weed-free as possible and mark out beds and rows before beginning. Plant seeds to the depth and spacing recommended on the seed packages, although if you're planting in mid-season, you may want to put them in slightly deeper to prevent them from drying out in the summer sun.

Getting small seeds into the soil is sometimes tricky. Grass seed and other widely spread seeds can be broadcast by hand or by hand-held seed spreaders available at most garden centres. But evenly distributing tiny seeds such as carrots along a furrow can be more of a challenge. I find the most effective method is to mix them with dry sand and then sow them. Some small seeds, like radish, are best tapped directly from the packet. Retailers offer a variety of inexpensive hand-held devices that make distributing seeds evenly much easier.

I like to cover the seeds with a thin layer of vermiculite, worm castings or sand after planting; it marks the rows and also helps to prevent the soil from crusting over after a rainfall or during a dry spell (this crust can hinder the seedlings' growth and also make water absorption more difficult). Water the beds lightly with a fine spray so as not to disturb freshly planted seeds, but keep the soil moist to hasten germination and prevent the seeds from dehydrating.

SOWING SEEDS

1. Use a string line to mark out rows before digging.

2. Dig a shallow furrow to the correct depth.

3. Mix small seeds with sand for easier distribution.

4. Cover seeds with a layer of vermiculite after planting.

Seed tape keeps seeds evenly spaced.

MAKE YOUR OWN SEED TAPE
Create a sure-fire straight row of seeds by making your own seed tapes. This is an excellent project for children. Simply roll out toilet paper on a kitchen counter. Place seeds evenly along the middle third of paper. A dab of flour/water solution will hold the seeds in place. Fold the toilet paper over the seeds from both sides, then fold or roll the paper for easy carrying. Unfold or unroll the seed tape on the prepared ground, then sprinkle loose soil over the tape to the appropriate depth and water well.

PLANTING ANNUALS & PERENNIALS

Early morning or late afternoon is my favourite time for planting annual bedding plants and perennials. This keeps the plants out of the strong midday sun and ensures that the water you give them during and after planting won't evaporate so quickly. Planting on overcast days also works well and, while some gardeners advise against working in the rain, I've never experienced problems planting in wet conditions other than an accumulation of mud on my boots. In fact, U.K. gardeners would never be able to do much if they could work only in dry weather!

HARDENING OFF

If you are planting newly purchased bedding plants (including tomato transplants) or perennials in a sunny location, introduce them gradually to the full sun by putting out the trays or flats of transplants in the morning and late afternoon sun for a day or two, and gradually increase the time they spend in full sun over a period of one week. This is especially important if you are planting in early spring, when greenhouse-grown bedding plants are "soft" and not quite ready for the harsh realities of the outdoors.

When you keep plants in trays for a day or more, make sure they stay well hydrated. *It is an excellent idea to water your bedding plants with a compost tea solution before planting them as this will help to establish roots quickly when their root balls hit the soil.*

Plant perennials once the soil has reached a temperature of at least 5°C (40°F) and annuals in soil that is 15° to 20°C (60° to 70°F), though pansies and violas can be planted in cooler soil. Most young plants have been growing in a warm greenhouse, and cold soil can give the roots a shock and set the plants back.

If the entire bed has been dug over and the soil loosened, the holes for individual plants need only be slightly wider than the root ball. If you are "pocket planting" in an existing bed, try to make the width of the planting hole considerably wider than the root mass. Dig planting holes 15 to 20 centimetres (six to eight inches) deep and amend the soil if necessary with generous quantities of compost and/or well-rotted manure. The mix should be about half topsoil/half compost. Don't be afraid to mix the existing garden soil with the compost or composted manure.

Water the planting holes before adding the plants to ensure that the roots get immediate access to moisture. Space most annuals 20 to 25 centimetres (eight to 10 inches) apart to allow for growth. Edging plants such as alyssum, ageratum and lobelia can be planted closer together for a denser look, while large-growing annuals such as geraniums, cleome and tall marigolds can be set farther apart.

Impatiens are reliable annuals for a shady spot.

Newly planted bedding plants will soon fill in and grow together.

Follow the directions provided by the nursery on how far apart to space specific perennials—always taking into account the plant's mature height and spread. Plant tags now provide much of the cultural information you'll need. When removing potted plants of any kind from their container, turn the container over and push gently on the bottom. If necessary, you can run a clean knife between the pot and the soil to loosen the plants. Resist the temptation to pull the plant from the pot by the stem as this can damage it. (I can't tell you how many times I have done this and regretted it crouched in the garden with soil and roots in one hand and the top of the plant in the other).

For most container—grown plants, the roots can simply be left as they are, although I like to loosen them by gently pulling them apart, particularly if the plant seems root-bound in the pot. Tuck the plant in the prepared hole and firm the soil gently around the root ball —you want to press firmly enough that there are no air pockets around the roots, but not so hard that you compact the soil.

The OxyBubbler water breaker delivers fresh oxygen-rich water.

Once in the ground, new plantings need to be kept moist but not water-logged. Regular, gentle watering is necessary. I like to use a water wand or water breaker—the soft flow of water is ideal. After planting annuals, keep the soil moist for the first two weeks as they put their roots down. Perennials need to be generously watered for their first full growing season. Check the specific types of plants described in this chapter for more details about watering. Of course, no newly planted plant likes bog-like conditions. Let the soil be your guide—push your finger into it from time to time and, when it is dry a centimetre or two down, water enough to ensure that moisture has percolated down to the root zone.

1. Support the base of the plant with your hand at soil level.

2. Tip container over while gently pushing on the bottom.

3. Plant and root ball will release from container and must be supported.

4. A healthy root system should be planted immediately before the soil dries out.

A scalloped- shaped, wire support, ideal for tall plants.

A twine grid is easy to make.

A pigtail plant support works well for tall perennials.

SUPPORT YOUR LOCAL PLANTS

What is sadder than going into the garden to find a delphinium with its gorgeous blooms hanging limply off a snapped stem? For very tall flowers such as delphiniums, lupines, foxgloves, gladioli, hollyhocks, bearded irises and lilies, some support is often necessary if they are to make it through their blooming season undamaged.

Even if a plant is not top-heavy when in bloom, it may require some form of support if its stems tend to bend over or it is in a windy, exposed site. There are many commercial plant supports available—from single-stem supports, to stakes with attached wire loops that can prop a number of stems, to link stakes that fasten together to form a cage or are attached to a small grid that can hold up several plants at one time.

Keep the following mind as you provide support to your tall perennials, vines, tomatoes and roses:

• A plant should be allowed some movement—gently swaying in a breeze helps strengthen stems. When tying plants to the support, leave some room between the stake and the stem.

• Keep stakes far enough away from the base of the plant to avoid damaging the roots.

• Support a plant while it is still small. Attaching stakes or putting a support around a mature plant is cumbersome and awkward. In my garden, mid-June through early July is prime "staking time." Besides, by mid-June most of the planting is done, affording you a little more time for this job. (Staking is a good excuse to inspect your plants close-up too).

• Stakes should reach to just below the flower spikes, so keep the mature height of the plant in mind when putting in the supports.

• Stakes are easiest to put in when the soil is slightly moist.

One of the best ways to deal with a group of tall blooms is to create a grid from twine and narrow stakes. In the early spring before the plants have begun to really take off, place the stakes (garden centres often carry green-dyed bamboo stakes that virtually disappear among the flower stalks) around the perimeter of the plants. Use four stakes to create a square, or more if covering a large area. Thread green garden twine around the outside of the stakes (wrap it around each stake a few times to prevent slipping) and then crisscross the twine between the stakes to create a loose grid. Do this at several heights and add another level of twine if the plants grow very tall over the course of the summer.

The twine grid, above center, was made with jute twine and natural wood stakes to clearly show how it's done, but coloured stakes and twine will practically disappear as the plants fill in.

The plants will grow up through the grid and, as long as you have made the horizontal spaces large enough, the plants will have room to move in the breeze but won't fall over if they are buffeted by strong winds or get too top-heavy.

PLANTING A TREE

1. Dig a planting hole twice the width of the root ball.

2. Add compost to the planting hole to improve soil texture.

3. Plant tree slightly higher than soil level in container to allow room for mulch.

4. Gently step on the soil around the base of the tree to lightly compact soil and remove air pockets. Mulch and water well.

PLANTING TREES & SHRUBS

So-called "nursery stock" (trees, shrubs, evergreens, roses and even large perennials grown in containers or balled and burlapped in the growing field) can be planted at any time of the day and in virtually any weather, as long as you remember that:

- No plant will perform well if you allow it to sit in the sun to dry out before planting.
- All plants benefit from a well-prepared planting hole.

If you cannot plant for a few days or more after taking delivery of nursery stock, it is best stored on the shady side of your home and hand-watered as the top two centimetres (3/4 inch) of soil become dry. Windy weather will necessitate more frequent watering. Different plants will have different watering needs, so check the tags.

When preparing the new home for your tree, don't be stingy with the size of the hole. (I refer to trees here, but the planting instructions are essentially the same for shrubs and conifers.) It should be at least two to three times as wide as the root ball or the nursery pot, and slightly deeper than the root ball or pot. Once the hole is dug, check its drainage. If the drainage is poor, you may have to break up and amend the soil in the hole and the surrounding area.

Remember that the root system of a mature tree will cover a large area. If you enrich just the soil in the planting hole, the roots may be reluctant to grow past the amended area and, if they do, they may experience shock or simply push up to the surface. Ideally, the whole planting area should be amended with lots of compost. If you are not prepared to amend the soil to the breadth of the dripline, check with your local nursery about what tree would thrive in your existing soil conditions (see Chapter 13 for more about knowing your soil).

If your soil is clay-based, pierce the inside walls of the hole with a fork so that the tree roots will be able to grow through it more easily. Add water to the hole before putting the tree in.

Bare-root trees should be planted as soon as possible after you get them home, and should never be allowed to dry out. Keep them heeled in (that is, with the roots buried in soil temporarily) until you can plant them. Soak the roots thoroughly before planting. Make a mound of soil in the middle of the hole and place the tree or shrub on top, spreading the roots over the mound. This will prevent air pockets around the roots. Roots should be loosened and spread apart to encourage straight, even root growth. Very long roots can be trimmed to fit the hole. Prune any that appear broken or discoloured.

Trees and shrubs in fibre or peat pots can be planted pot and all, but slit the sides of the pot top to bottom in three or four places, and cut off the rim so it doesn't wick water out of the soil. It's a good idea to soak the pot in water before planting.

If the tree has been grown in a plastic container, it must be removed before planting, keeping the root ball intact. Try to leave the dirt surrounding the roots undisturbed to reduce trauma to your tree. However, if the plant is root-bound—i.e., it is a mass of roots circling around on themselves—loosen the roots and spread them outward, or make shallow cuts down the sides of the root ball to encourage outward growth. Plant a container-grown plant to the same depth it was growing in the pot.

If planting a tree in an exposed site, set the tree so that it leans about five degrees toward the direction of the prevailing wind, even though you are going to stake it after planting. It will straighten as it grows and not appear to be bending backward in a strong wind when it is young and supple.

Mulch the root zone, but keep the mulch away from the trunk.

After placing the tree in its hole, fill halfway with soil and water thoroughly. Let the water drain, then finish filling the hole, gently firming the soil around the roots so there are no air pockets.

Once the hole is filled, heap some soil to make a crater or basin encircling the base of the tree at the edge of the roots' reach. Fill this basin with water immediately and again in a few days. For the rest of the season, water as the soil becomes dry two to four centimetres (one to 1 1/2 inches) down. Add a layer of organic matter five to six centimetres (two to 2 1/2 inches) deep as a mulch over the entire root zone, but not touching the base of the tree, to reduce evaporation and prevent competition from weeds. Water your new tree deeply before the ground freezes for the winter to protect the roots from freeze-thaw cycles.

Well-mulched, staked and wrapped, this tree just needs regular watering to get it off to the best start.

Stake trees planted in a windy, exposed spot or if the tree is very top-heavy or taller than 60 centimetres (two feet). If you do stake your tree using a single stake, be sure to place it on the west side of the tree, bracing it against the pull of the prevailing winds.

For a large tree, it is best to use three stakes at regular intervals, 60 to 90 centimetres (two to three feet) away from the tree. They should be inserted at least 25 centimetres (10 inches) into the ground. Before attaching heavy guy wire to the stakes, cover the ends of the wire where it will loop around the trunk with lengths of rubber tubing (old hose works well) so the wire doesn't damage the bark.

Wrap the trunks of young fruit and flowering trees with a rodent-proof plastic tree wrap (not just any old plastic) or tar-impregnated crepe paper to protect the trunks from winter damage and animals.

Apply a spiral plastic tree wrap in fall to protect against rodent damage.

We love tulips in spring, but so do deer and squirrels!

I love the flowers of spring-flowering bulbs such as daffodil, crocus, tulip and hyacinth. These bulbs are planted in the fall and stay in the ground from year to year. They are so winter-hardy that literally every Canadian gardener can grow them.

PLANTING BULBS

Summer-blooming bulbs like gladioli, tuberous begonias, dahlias and canna lilies (though not technically bulbs) are planted in spring and also produce beautiful flowers.

They usually need to be lifted from the ground in the fall and stored indoors over winter.

WHEN IS A BULB NOT A BULB?

Bulb - hyacinth, tulip and daffodils.
Rhizome - iris, lily of the valley and canna lily.
Corm - crocus, gladiolus.
Tuber - begonia and anemone.

Although their forms may differ, these are all generally categorized as bulbs.

Summer- flowering dahlias grow from tubers.

Most bulbs like neutral to mildly acidic soil that is loose and well drained. The general rule is to plant bulbs three times as deep as the bulb is thick, measured from top to bottom (and always plant bulbs with the pointy side up).

Usually this means small bulbs like crocus and scilla are covered with 1.25 to 2.5 centimetres (1/2 to one inch) of soil, and large tulip and daffodil bulbs with 15 to 20 centimetres (six to eight inches) of soil. If your soil is clay-based, plant more shallowly than normal to help prevent the bulbs from rotting.

Bulbs can be planted more deeply if squirrels and other small animals are a problem, but small bulbs may have to concentrate on root and foliage growth at the expense of blossoms if planted too deep. In Zone 4 and colder, bulbs should be planted a bit more deeply than the "three times" rule would suggest, as intense freezing and sudden cold snaps may damage them. In these climates, it is helpful to mulch bulbs with 30 centimetres (12 inches) of fallen leaves or three to five centimetres (one to two inches) of finely ground pine or cedar bark.

1. Dig a planting hole three times as deep as the bulb is thick.

2. Amend the soil with sharp sand to improve drainage.

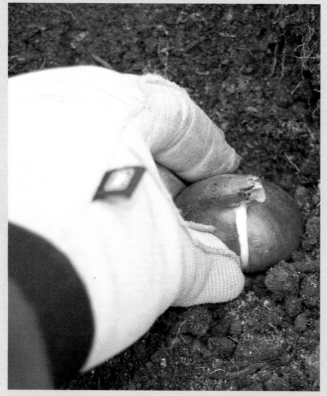

3. Place bulbs in the hole and twist gently to make sure they are in contact with the soil.

4. Fill the planting hole with loosened soil. Firm gently with your foot to remove air pockets and water deeply.

Space bulbs by at least three centimetres (1 1/4" inches) apart so any disease can't spread through the whole lot.

The deeper bulbs are planted the more critical the need for good drainage (many bulbs are susceptible to fungus and mildew diseases). If your soil is heavy, dig in generous quantities of sharp sand to improve drainage. Your goal should be about 1/3 sand to 2/3 top soil. Soil should be moist but not wet before planting.

Rhizomes and plants with short tubers, like begonia, need to be planted so their tops are level with the surface of the soil. The rhizomes of iris should be no more than 2.5 centimetres (one inch) deep, and the top third to half of the rhizome can actually be above the soil. Other tuberous roots (for example, daylily, dahlia and ranunculus) must be planted so that fibrous roots with the stem buds are near the surface.

Plant bulbs in groups in a wide hole or use a bulb-planting tool, dibbler or narrow trowel to cut holes for individual bulbs. If you are planting bulbs individually, space them twice the diameter of the bulbs apart to avoid overcrowding. Remember, flowers from bulbs look best if planted in groups or wide swaths. When the bulbs are set in the soil, it is important that the root end, called the basal plate, is in direct contact with soil; don't leave air pockets under or around the bulbs when the holes are filled with soil.

Bulbs don't need any fertilizer the first year; subsequently, an annual application of compost or well-rotted manure when shoots are emerging in spring and then again in fall is all they need.

I enjoy planting bulbs in layers with larger bulbs on the bottom and smaller bulbs on top. Not only does this make maximum use of a small space, but if you choose bulbs that bloom at different times, the successive blooms will cover the spent foliage of earlier flowers.

Grow hyacinths for their intensely sweet fragrance. The colour is a bonus.

Some of my 12,000 naturalized 'Carlton' daffodils that grow and improve each year in our yard.

NATURALIZING BULBS

Many hardy bulbs can be planted so they naturalize—that is, multiply and spread naturally throughout an area. Crocuses, grape hyacinths and scilla are all good choices for naturalizing. Hyacinths, irises and daffodils often spread from season to season, but they do so more slowly, especially in dry or cold climates. To create a natural look in a lawn or beneath trees, scatter bulbs by the handful across the area. Then, using a sharp spade or shovel, open up the turf or soil and plant the bulbs where they fell (they will come up through the turf next spring). If you do plant bulbs in a grassy area, remember that, once the flowers are finished, the leaves should not be cut or removed for several weeks, as they are feeding the bulbs (by converting the energy of the sun into plant "sugars") for future flower production. Corms are less reliant on foliage, so plants like crocus and scilla can be cut earlier and are therefore excellent choices for lawns.

Note that not all bulb varieties are suitable for naturalizing. Look for bulbs that are labelled as such, ask for advice when buying, or visit my website for lists of my favourite bulbs used for this purpose—www.markcullen.com.

You can't beat daffodils for early colour and for cutting.

The compost bin is an invaluable recycler.

Remember that every gardener has lost some plants for one reason or another at planting time —and often there is no logical explanation either! These are good times to remind yourself that there are no failures in the garden, just composting opportunities.

TRICKING THE SQUIRRELS

Anyone who has experienced an invigorating fall afternoon planting bulbs will also, no doubt, have experienced the annoyance of watching squirrels cheerfully carrying away those bulbs a few days later. Take heart—there are a number of ways of protecting bulbs from squirrels and other rodents.

- BLOOD MEAL. Dug in and around the bulbs, it often discourages squirrels, although raccoons find it tasty.

- CHICKEN WIRE. Place chicken wire or loose plastic mesh, covered with mulch, over the soil surface to protect the bulbs beneath. Remove the chicken wire in the spring if it is covering large bulbs.

- PAPER BAGS. I have had good luck planting tulip bulbs in paper bags, which hide some of the bulb odour from the foraging squirrels in fall and will rot by spring.

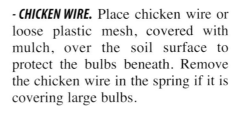

Chicken wire used to protect a new planting!

- OYSTER SHELLS. Spread broken oyster or clam shells or crushed eggshells over the bulbs when planting. Rodents dislike digging through the shells.

- ORGANIC REPELLENTS. There are a number of safe, organic rodent repellents in granular and liquid forms on the market. I use them in the spring and summer, but find them particularly helpful in fall when I spray a little on top of my bulbs at planting time, just before covering them with soil.

- DAFFODILS. The one foolproof solution is to plant just daffodils. They're toxic and squirrels hate them. You can also plant daffodils among or encircling more vulnerable bulbs to help discourage predators.

- GET A DOG. It's not foolproof, but a good dog (even a small one!) can do a remarkable job of keeping rodents at bay. Even the smell of a dog can deter some rodents.

Armed with some knowledge of what plants like and do not like when it comes time for planting, you can achieve a success rate that you never imagined. Truth is, many plants are very forgiving, and those that are not will send you signs (like yellowing leaves, droopy leaves and lacklustre performance) indicating that changes at the root zone are required.

My father, Len Cullen, standing by the "family" tree that he planted in 1955, located at the home of the Hockey Hall of Fame, Toronto, Ontario.

I LOVE TO DIG!

(*A special excerpt from A Sandbox of a Different Kind*, by Mark Cullen)

I had the privilege of growing up with gardening. My dad, Len, had a passion for it that almost defied description. He was, after all, the only person I know of who kissed evergreens— all the time! Without apology.

One day in 1986, when I was barely 30, I took a walk with Dad through the valley of his public show garden, Cullen Gardens and Miniature Village in Whitby, Ontario. It was one of those lovely early fall days when the temperature is perfect to be outdoors. There were no bugs to speak of, which was really something in that mosquito-infested cedar forest. We just walked and talked. Him, walking with his favourite D-handled spade, and me, just trying to keep up the pace of both the conversation and the walk.

On most such occasions, our conversations revolved almost exclusively around business. Even the topic of gardening was always discussed in the context of the family business. So it came as a great surprise to me on this particular day when he stopped abruptly during our stroll, mid-stride. He bent down, took a stance that I had seen thousands of times before, and he began to dig. Right in the middle of the dirt path. One spadeful. A second. A third. Then he moved the dirt back into the new hole with the spade.

He slowly straightened his back, hand on the bottom of his spine for support. Slightly out of breath, he said, "I love to dig." Then he paused. "I *love* to dig," he said again. Then he looked me square in the eye and exclaimed in case I hadn't heard him, "I LOVE to dig, Mark!"

Wow, I thought. My dad really is kind of nuts.

Expressing such passion over a basic thing like digging was unusual even for him. There was no doubt in my mind that he was good at it. There is a particular skill to digging. The position of your feet, the spacing of your arms on the shaft of the spade, the thrust of the blade into the ground, pushing your shoulders into it… all factor into a satisfying digging experience. Not to mention that the spade itself must be clean, and sharp as a butcher knife, and it helps if it is worn with use—the oils from your hands having smoothed the wooden shaft to a working finish. This is a tool without a price, because you can't buy one. You create it through practice.

After our memorable digging experience, about 10 or 12 years went by. It took this long for me to begin to understand what he was talking about that autumn day in the valley.

Over that time, I had planned and planted my own garden— a few times. I had learned to take the time to slow down and dig my own soil. To smell it in the moist spring, the hot, dry summer and the coolness of autumn.

I had spent many autumn days turning finished compost into my garden soil. I rescued more than a few earthworms from the blade of my spade. And I would rest on the D-handle of it after a good dig.

Time and practice caused the experience of digging to slowly sink into my being… until one day I got it. There is a great joy to digging soil.

Today, there is an English spade hanging in my tool shed that I treasure above all of my garden tools. It has a fine metal blade that holds an edge when sharpened; made of Sheffield steel, it bends rather than breaks when pressured.

My Dad's favourite D-handled shovel.

It slices through soil like a hot knife through butter. It is such a favourite of mine that it has appeared in more of my TV shows than my kids have. And they don't make them any more (the spade, of course, not the kids).

One of the most difficult decisions I will have to make someday is which of our four kids I will leave this spade to. The spade given to me by my dad the day I left home.

Perhaps one day, while walking and talking about ordinary things with one of our precious children, or perhaps while digging, it will come to me. Just as my dad opened my eyes to something that I had always considered ordinary, the soil will speak to me.

And I will know just what to do.

(Excerpted from A Sandbox of a Different Kind by Mark Cullen, Mark's Choice, 2007.)

Water conservation is not only about "if" but also "when" and "how".

CHAPTER FIFTEEN

Conserving Water

Travelling through the English countryside where the great swaths of uncultivated meadows and the strips of untended roadside are a verdant green, you realize how much toil an abundance of rain can take out of a gardener's life! As a Canadian, all you have to do is look to certain parts of our West Coast (like Tofino) to see the upside of a drizzly spring and summer. Gardeners in many parts of Canada have to "put up" with warm summer sunshine and a significant number of dry, clear days each growing season.

Not a burden really, but it does keep most of us occupied with watering our gardens.

I find that I am asked the same questions about watering repeatedly on my radio phone-in show. How much? When? How often? And there's a fourth common question, not always asked directly, but often implied: "How can I do less watering?"

Watering consumes time but also one of our most precious resources. Plants need water to maintain cell structure and continue growth and photosynthesis. Their roots can only absorb soil nutrients when those nutrients are dissolved in water. Even a very fertile soil will do a plant little good if the earth is completely dried out.

While water is essential to the health and beauty of your garden, overwatering does more harm than good. It starves the soil and your plants of vital oxygen and can cause significant

Many of the questions that I field on my radio show relate to watering issues.

problems. Given the choice between a dry or an overwatered lawn or garden, I usually will take the dry one. Plants generally can adapt better to this situation and it's easier to fix.

Turn your in-ground watering system on to the "manual" setting.

THE DIRT ON IN-GROUND WATERING SYSTEMS

I often say that programmed in-ground lawn and garden sprinklers are a plant's biggest enemy. Not that I am against these in-ground systems—far from it. They can be an efficient method of applying water where it is needed most. What I object to is how many people—and businesses—use them.

Have you ever noticed automatic sprinkler systems in your neighbourhood that keep on watering, often daily, with no regard for recent rainfall or local watering restrictions? Not only is this a waste of water but I have also seen an otherwise successful garden literally drowning as a result.

If you have an in-ground watering system, I recommend that you:

• Turn OFF the automatic feature of the system.

• Turn ON the manual feature.

When your garden is dry to about two centimetres below the soil surface, turn the system on for about two hours in either the morning or evening (midday watering will lose up to 30 percent to evaporation).

If your lawn has not received significant rainfall in seven days, apply water from your in-ground system for two to three hours in the morning (preferably) or evening (as a second choice).

In a drought situation, do not apply water to your lawn. Let it go dormant—it will recover nicely when evening temperatures cool off to below 20°C and the rains return.

Often, the best moisture meter is your finger!

One good way to gauge the need for water is to push your finger into the soil. If it is dry below 2.5 centimetres (one inch), your garden needs watering. If the soil crumbles and will not hold shape when you squeeze a handful, you need to water.

HOW OFTEN AND HOW MUCH TO WATER

Knowing how often and how much to water is based on understanding your plants' moisture requirements and your soil's ability to retain moisture. Remember that newly installed plants need more frequent watering than established plants, which have deeper roots and better access to ground moisture. Water new plants as the soil becomes dry to the touch, and give them extra water for up to a year.

Plants around the foundation of your home will probably need extra water, too, because houses are usually constructed with excellent drainage around their foundations to keep water well away.

Careful observation of your garden is helpful, but you can't always rely on a plant's appearance to tell you it needs watering. If some plants look wilted in the heat of the day, it may simply be that the leaves are transpiring (i.e., giving off moisture along with oxygen) more quickly than the plant can take up water from the roots. Once the sun goes off them, they perk up and look normal

However, some plants do serve as accurate indicators. Hydrangeas and dogwoods will droop when they need water. For many plants, droopy leaves are not harmful in the short term, providing you pay attention and give them a drink.

The hotter and/or the windier the weather, the more water your garden requires. The soil dries out more quickly and plants transpire more (although some plants react to strong winds by stopping transpiration for a time).

My rule of thumb for watering both gardens and lawns is to water deeply— 2.5 centimetres (one inch) of water will usually provide moisture for a 30-centimetre (one-foot) depth of healthy soil —usually no more than once a week. You want to have at least 20 to 22.5 centimetres (eight to nine inches) of moist soil.

Infrequent but generous watering forces the roots of plants to grow deeper in search of moisture, without starving them for water. Deep roots mean that your plants can better survive short periods of drought and that those roots are protected should the soil surface heat up in very sunny, hot conditions.

Unfortunately, no one can tell you exactly how long to run that sprinkler to water your garden sufficiently. Each sprinkler or irrigation system is different; each soil type retains a different amount of water. To check how much water your system is distributing in a given period of time, try the following simple test.

Hydrangea shrubs are excellent natural barometers of soil moisture, when leaves wilt—time to water! Forsythia and dogwood also work well.

This Mark's Choice sprinkler uses 30 percent less water due to the fine droplets of water it produces.

Take a small, shallow can and mark a 2.5-centimetre (one-inch) depth line on it. Place it on the lawn or soil. Start your sprinkler or watering system and time how long it takes for the can to fill up to the mark. Now you know how many minutes it takes to apply 2.5-centimetres (one-inch) of water.

Next, you must determine how much of the water you apply actually stays in the soil. Sandy soil drains quickly and has more difficulty retaining moisture. You will need to leave the water running longer to achieve the same effect that a shorter watering spell would have on organically enriched loam. This is just one of many good reasons

A shallow can collects water.

to incorporate generous quantities of compost into your garden soil (see Chapter 13 for more on soil amending).

DRAINAGE TESTS
Good drainage is crucial to plant health. Poor drainage results in water-logged, oxygen-starved soil. Really quick drainage means dry soil and fewer nutrients getting to the plants. To test your drainage, dig a hole 15-centimetres (six-inches) wide and 30-centimetres (one foot) deep.

Fill it with water and let drain. Fill it again and time how long it takes to empty. If the water takes more than half an hour to drain from the hole, you have drainage problems, perhaps due to compaction or high clay content. If water drains from the hole in minutes or right before your eyes, there is no drainage problem; indeed, it might even be too fast-draining. (Remember that planting time, particularly if you're putting in a large tree or shrub, gives you the ideal opportunity to perform a drainage test in the planting hole.)

To further test if your soil drains too quickly, water an area very deeply, giving it at least five centimetres (two inches) of water. After two days, dig

down in that spot 15 centimetres (six inches). If the soil is already dry to the bottom, it is probably draining too quickly.

IMPROVING DRAINAGE
• *Sandy soil.* Amend with compost or composted cattle manure to improve moisture retention.
• *Heavy clay soil.* Amend with compost, well-rotted manure and sharp sand to improve drainage and air circulation.

A timed drainage test.

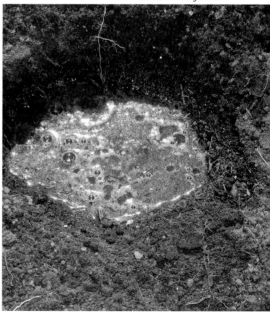

Red twig dogwood enjoys moisture.

Sedum is drought-tolerant.

Daylilies do not demand a lot of water once established.

• *Hardpan.* Break up hardpan (a very hard, compacted layer of soil, usually clay) in the top 60 centimetres (two feet) of soil by double-digging (see Chapter 14 for how to double-dig). Digging in lots of fallen leaves in autumn can help a lot. I also recommend planting sweet clover as its long roots can penetrate hardpan, and may be able to break up hard soil more than 120 centimetres (four feet) deep!

If your hardpan requires a pickaxe to break it up, you really should consider replacing the soil that is there with good-quality triple mix.

If amending the soil or digging it out is too onerous, consider creating a raised bed on top of the poorly draining area. Also, be careful not to overwater areas where drainage is sluggish.

WORK WITH WHAT YOU HAVE!

Use a soggy patch to create a bog garden, featuring plants such as red twig dogwood, turtlehead, bugbane and yellow flag iris that thrive with "wet feet." Alternatively, plant a dry area with drought-tolerant plants such as sedum, yarrow, daylily, many of the ornamental grasses and juniper that appreciate excellent drainage.

A raised bed is easier to hand-water, but dries out more quickly than a garden bed.

Sprinklers above ground should not be used on windy days.

WATERING WISELY

Water is best applied at a slow, consistent rate so the soil gets a chance to absorb the water before it runs off, puddles or evaporates.

WHEN TO WATER

My vote for the *best* time to water is always early morning. After a long, cool night, before the sun begins to heat up the air and the ground, there will be the least amount of evaporation. Also, in hot weather, the plants will be less stressed first thing in the morning. Avoid watering on a windy day, as air movement increases evaporation and that just wastes water.

My second choice is to water in the early evening, before it is really dark and cool.

Most trees, shrubs and evergreens need a thorough watering just before the ground freezes.

To avoid excess evaporation as the droplets travel through the air, water is best applied as close to the ground and the plants' root systems as possible. Most roots are found within 60 centimetres (two feet) of the surface (including roots that are most active in water and nutrient absorption and in respiration).

Many gardeners used to believe that the longest root grew no farther out than the widest branch of a tree or shrub, but everyone who has had the headache of tree roots growing in their sewer systems or underground pipes will tell you that some tree and shrub roots can travel much farther than that. Nevertheless, the drip line (that circle you would draw on the ground around a tree corresponding to the outermost edge of the tree's canopy) is a useful guide. Most roots grow within a metre (39 inches) of this circle, so always water to the full extent of the drip line.

When you are creating lawn areas or beds for your flowers, tree and shrubs, try to use shapes that correspond with the area covered by your water distribution system. Of course, you can change your irrigation system to cover the shapes of your beds, and soaker hoses are useful for getting into corners where sprinklers can't reach.

SOAKER HOSES AND SPRINKLERS

With tiny perforations along their length, soaker hoses provide a slow, steady supply of water directly to the soil. I have had excellent results using them in the vegetable garden (where I am planting in long rows), in areas of full sun and on newly planted trees, shrubs and roses. Soaker hoses are long and flexible and can be threaded through your plants and along rows of vegetables. Since the hose is laid on the soil or just under it and it is usually shaded by the foliage, you can safely water pretty well any time of day. Another reason to use a soaker hose? It frequently is made of recycled rubber. Not a bad use for old tires!

A soaker hose, made from recycled rubber.

Sprinkler hoses are long, slightly flattened rubber or plastic hoses with a series of small holes along their length. Like soaker hoses, they can be threaded through gardens and even along lawns. If laid with the holes facing down, the sprinkler hose acts much like a soaker hose and can be mulched over. Placed with the holes facing up, the hose sprays water to a larger area, but some water will be lost to evaporation.

A sprinkler hose.

A soaker hose, made from recycled rubber.

The traditional oscillating sprinkler, which moves back and forth, is fun for children to run through but it can lose up to an astonishing 50 percent of its water through evaporation when used in the middle of the day.

While these sprinklers cover large areas, they may spray more water at either end of their arc as they pause to change direction. Some models have new features to address uneven water distribution, so check with your garden centre if you have concerns, and use them in the early morning to limit evaporation.

XERISCAPING AND WATER CONSERVATION

Xeriscaping is a topic that is cropping up more frequently in gardening magazines and at horticultural shows, as well as in the conversations of gardeners. It is a relatively new gardening approach that can be adapted to suit various climates and terrains.

The term itself is from the Greek word *xeros* meaning dry, and literally means "dry scene." In practice, today's xeriscaping is not about creating a desert-like habitat, or vistas of brush, cacti and gravel. Nor is xeriscaping now about the exclusive use of drought-tolerant plants (the original xeriscape was designed for gardens in the western United States). It is about gardening with less water, and it dovetails very nicely with both low-maintenance gardening approaches and ecologically responsible water conservation.

Xeriscaping is especially useful if you live in areas where nature does not provide a lot of moisture during the growing season or if you are gardening on a slope. It also means less maintenance because, in addition to saving watering time, many of its techniques help reduce weeds, and many drought-tolerant plants tend to have fewer pests (their foliage is less tasty).

But there are other pressing reasons to employ xeriscaping techniques. Household water consumption and water supply have become urgent issues for many regions. While Canada boasts the most fresh water per square kilometre in the world, water treatment for household use is extremely costly, driven higher by our penchant for wasting vast quantities of the precious resource. The days when city-dwellers could crank up water consumption with little effect on expenses are quickly drawing to a close.

If you rely on a well for your water supply, you no doubt have an awareness of water consumption that the rest of us are just beginning to appreciate. For you, many of the xeriscaping approaches may already be second nature.

Xeriscaping provides a host of benefits, and its water-saving principles are simple, straightforward and easy to accomplish:

MULCH
One of the basic tenets of xeriscaping, mulch holds moisture in the soil and reduces the need for watering, among many other positive effects. (See Chapter 16 for more on mulch.)

GROUP PLANTS WITH SIMILAR WATERING NEEDS TOGETHER
If all the drought-tolerant plants are in one area, and the water-lovers in another, you can avoid overwatering the less thirsty plants and eliminate the hassle of giving different watering regimes to individual plants within a bed—saving both water and time.

WATER DEEPLY BUT LESS FREQUENTLY
As previously discussed, frequent watering is as bad for your plants as it is for your water supply. Remember that all plants require at least a brief period of dryness between watering.

A well-mulched garden uses up to 70 percent less water.

The OxyBubbler water wand.

WATER THE SOIL, NOT THE ATMOSPHERE
Even when hand watering, try to get the moisture to the soil as directly as possible and avoid systems that spray water where it isn't needed or let it puddle or run off.

USE WATER-EFFICIENT DELIVERY MEANS
Low-spraying sprinklers, soaker or sprinkler hoses or a manually controlled in-ground system make the best use of water.

IMPROVE THE SOIL
With gardening, it's always about the soil, isn't it? The most water-efficient garden is one with rich, fertile soil that drains adequately, but not too quickly. See page 175 for more on drainage and Chapter 13 for ways to improve your soil.

SLOW DOWN WATER FLOW ON SLOPES
Slopes are naturally difficult to keep adequately watered and can result in wasteful runoff. To save water and keep plantings in good shape:

• Use drought-tolerant plants on the high points of a slope and moisture-loving plants at the bottom where the water drains.

• Create circular depressions or basins around plants on the slope so the water will gather around the root zone. On large slopes, shallow horizontal or angled ditches or swales can be created at intervals to collect water and slow drainage, or channel water to the plantings.

• Plant drought-tolerant groundcovers to slow water runoff and reduce soil erosion.

CREATE WATER-HOLDING BEDS
If you have plants that require quite a lot of water and your soil isn't particularly water retentive, line beds with layered newspaper or even the plastic sheeting used for bog gardens to help keep water in the soil. Dig down 30 to 45 centimetres (12 to 18 inches), cover the base of the bed with your barrier material (it can extend up the sides, stopping about 15 centimetres/ six inches from the top), and fill the bed with rich, humusy soil. You can amend the existing soil with compost or well-rotted manure or replace it altogether with triple mix.

REDUCE THE USE OF RAISED BEDS
In sites with soggy soil, raised beds are an ideal way to improve drainage as water evaporates from the sides as well as the top of the bed. But in gardens without drainage problems, they are natural water hogs. In a xeriscape, raised beds should be only 10 to 15 centimetres (four to six inches) above ground level. Amend the soil to a depth of 45 centimetres (18 inches) to improve water retention.

CREATE WINDBREAKS
Planting shelter belts is a long-established prairie practice. These lines of trees and shrubs break the flow of wind as it crosses open areas, reducing evaporation, wind damage to plants and crops, and soil erosion on the leeward side of the plantings. Use this principle in the wind-exposed areas of your own garden. Plant attractive hedges, a cluster of trees and shrubs, a fence or a vine-covered trellis to break the path of the wind. The leeward side is cool and shady (and water-saving) so study the wind patterns carefully before siting the windbreak.

Portulaca is a drought-tolerant annual.

COLLECT RAINWATER:

How many times have you been out watering your garden only days after a heavy shower sent water flowing down the street into the storm sewers? Capture this water with a rain barrel, which collects the runoff from your roof. A variety of barrels are now available, and newer models offer various ways to direct the water to your garden and to keep overflow away from your house foundation. A screen on the top of the barrel prevents mosquitoes.

The rain barrel's advantages are:

• *Warm water. Do you like a cold shower? Well, like people, plants—especially container grown annuals and perennials—respond much better to warm water.*

• *Oxygen. Rain picks up 30 to 40 percent oxygen on its way down to earth; oxygen-rich water is better for everything you grow.*

• *"Teapot." Put a cloth bag 1/2 filled with compost in your rain barrel and let it steep for a day or more. The resulting "tea" is an excellent organic fertilizer for all plants!*

• *Convenience. It's much easier to fill a bucket or watering can from the rain barrel than it is to drag out the garden hose.*

Mark's Choice downspout extender.

REDIRECT AND/OR EXTEND DOWNSPOUTS

If your downspout disappears into the ground (to hook up with the city storm drains), disconnect it and redirect it to empty on your lawn or near your flower beds. Downspout extensions (plastic, stone or brick troughs) can also help get the water to your plants.

USE NEW PATIOS, DRIVEWAYS AND PATHS TO DIRECT RAINWATER

Build hardscaping features with a slight slope so they send rainwater to your lawn and garden instead of the street.

CHOOSE DROUGHT-TOLERANT PLANTS

You might be surprised to learn how many wonderfully attractive and versatile plants are drought-tolerant. Many, particularly native plants, are also pest- and disease-resistant.

Drought-tolerant plants are also ideal for sandy soil, areas with high elevation, hot southern or western exposures, on slopes, in open or windy spots, and near mature trees that absorb a lot of soil moisture. Remember, though, that these plants need regular watering their first year to get established, after which they will require less.

Big bluestem is a drought-tolerant native grass.

A rain barrel is handy, and plants love the water.

▲ Adam's needle.

▲ Black-eyed Susan.

▲ Blanket flower.

▲ Goldenrod.

DROUGHT - TOLERANT PLANTS

PERENNIALS

Adam's needle (*Yucca filamentosa*), Zone 4

Artemisia (*Artemisia*), Zone 2

Bearded iris (*Iris germanica*), Zone 3

Black-eyed Susan (*Rudbeckia*), Zone 4

Blanket flower (*Gaillardia*), Zone 3

Blazingstar (*Liatris*), Zone 3

Butterfly weed (*Asclepias tuberosa*), Zone 3

Common yarrow (*Achillea millefolium*), Zone 3

Crown vetch (*Coronilla varia*), Zone 3

Cushion spurge (*Euphorbia polychroma*), Zone 3

Daylily (*Hemerocallis*), Zone 3

Evening primrose (*Oenothera fruticosa*), Zone 5

False sunflower (*Heliopsis helianthoides*), Zone 4

Anise hyssop (*Agastache foeniculum*), Zone 5

Globe thistle (*Echinops*), Zone 4

Goldenrod (*Solidago*), Zone 3

Grey-headed coneflower (*Ratibida pinnata*), Zone 4

Hens and chicks (*Sempervivum*), Zone 3

Lance-leaved coreopsis (*Coreopsis lanceolata*), Zone 5

Lavender (*Lavandula*), Zone 5

Lily of the valley (*Convallaria*), Zone 2

Mother-of-thyme (*Thymus serpyllum*), Zone 3

Perennial alyssum, basket of gold (*Aurinia saxatilis*), Zone 4

Purple coneflower (*Echinacea purpurea*), Zone 3

Snow-in-summer (*Cerastium tomentosum*), Zone 2

Stonecrop (*Sedum*), Zone 3

Thrift (*Armeria*), Zone 5

ORNAMENTAL GRASSES

Big bluestem (*Andropogon gerardii*), Zone 3

Indian grass (*Sorghastrum nutans*), Zone 3

Switch grass (*Panicum virgatum*), Zone 3

▼ Stonecrop.   ▲ Purple coneflower.

DROUGHT - TOLERANT PLANTS

▲ *Ageratum.*

▲ *Marigold*

ANNUALS

Ageratum (*Ageratum houstonianum*)

Blanket flower (*Gaillardia puchella*)

Calendula (*Calendula officinalis*)

Cosmos (*Cosmos bipinnatus*)

Dusty miller (*Senecio cineraria*)

Flowering tobacco (*Nicotiana alata*)

Geranium (*Pelargonium*)

Marigold (*Tagetes*)

Ornamental kale (*Brassica oleracea*)

Petunia (*Petunia* x *hybrida*)

Portulaca (*Portulaca grandiflora*)

Salvia (*Salvia splendens*)

Snapdragon (*Antirrhinum majus*)

Statice (*Limonium*)

Sweet alyssum (*Lobularia maritima*)

Verbena (*Verbena*)

Zinnia (*Zinnia elegans)*

▲ *Cosmos.*

▲ *Petunia*

▼ *Geranium.*   ▲ *Dusty miller.*

▼ *Zinnia*   ▲ *Salvia.*

▲ Tulips.

DROUGHT - TOLERANT PLANTS

BULBS

Tulip (*Tulipa*)   Zone 3

TREES AND SHRUBS

Bayberry
(*Myrica pensylvanica*),   Zone 3

Bur oak
(*Quercus macrocarpa*),   Zone 2

Butterfly bush
(*Buddleja davidii*),   Zone 5

Caryopteris
(*Caryopteris* x
clandonensis),   Zone 5

Chokecherry
(*Prunus virginiana*),   Zone 3

Common juniper
(*Juniperus communis*),   Zone 3

Cotoneaster
(*Cotoneaster*),   Zone 5

Elder (*Sambucus*),   Zone 4

Hawthorn (*Crataegus*),   Zone 4

Honeysuckle
(*Lonicera japonica*),   Zone 3

Juniper (*Juniperus*),   Zone 3

Lilac (*Syringa*),   Zone 3

Nannyberry
(*Viburnum lentago*),   Zone 3

Oregon grape
(*Mahonia aquifolium*),   Zone 5

Pine (*Pinus*),   Zone 3

Rugosa rose
(*Rosa rugosa*),   Zone 3

Spruce (*Picea*),   Zone 2

Western sand cherry
(*Prunus besseyi*),   Zone 2

I get a lot of satisfaction out of planning and growing a garden that does not demand a lot of water. This also means that it will not demand a lot of my time.

Properly thought out and executed, a "low-water garden" may be the closest thing that you will get to a "low-maintenance" garden.

▲ Pine.

▲ Rugosa rose.

▲ Chokecherry.

▼ Lilac.

▼ Spruce.

There's nothing like mulch for gardening success and satisfaction.

CHAPTER SIXTEEN
Mulch

When people ask me the secret to successful gardening, I like to adapt that old real estate saying about location, and reply that the secret to a greener thumb lies in the three "m's" of gardening: mulch, mulch and mulch.

For me, one of the best jobs each spring is to pick up a few cubic yards of finely ground cedar bark mulch at the landscape supply yard in my pick up truck and spread a new layer of it over the

Wood chips create a nice mulched path.

A combination of pine needles and fallen leaves can make an attractive mulch in the country or cottage garden.

extensive paths throughout my garden. The job takes days when I do it myself and it is pure pleasure. I love the clean, earthy smell of the stuff, the texture of it as I push my mulching fork into it and, above all, the look of it as I spread it over the paths.

Of course, there is much more to good mulch than wonderful smells and tactile experiences. Mulching is so beneficial and serves so many different purposes that it is hard not to make it my number-one garden rule.

"I believe that 90 percent of gardening success is rooted in proper ground preparation and mulch is a major part of that."

BENEFITS OF MULCH

Mulch is the low-maintenance gardener's—indeed, any gardener's—secret weapon. Among its many benefits, mulch:

- If organic, will improve the nutrient content of the soil over time.
- Reduces weeding dramatically.
- Reduces water evaporation and the need to water.
- Protects the soil from temperature fluctuations.
- Can increase or decrease soil temperature (depending on the type of mulch).
- Prevents soil compaction and increases friability.

- Can reduce soil erosion, especially on slopes.
- Keeps dirt off the leaves of plants and veggies and therefore helps to suppress and control disease.
- Makes moving through your garden, especially the vegetable patch, easier—no muddy walkways.

INCREASED NUTRIENT CONTENT

As you learned in Chapter 13 about soil, organic material is a godsend for the garden. An organic mulch, especially one that breaks down relatively quickly, adds fresh organic material to your soil. As the mulch breaks down, earthworms pull the humus into the soil, aerating it as they go and producing castings that release valuable nutrients.

Organic material aids aeration, water percolation and enriches (depending on the type you choose) the soil with vital nutrients like nitrogen, phosphorus and potassium, as well as some trace elements. Decaying organic mulch promotes increased microbial activity, which makes potassium more readily available to plant roots.

A mulched pathway between perennials.

LESS WEEDING

As long as the mulch itself is weed-free—be careful of weed-filled hay, manure or plant material that has not been fully composted—it can prevent weed seeds from taking root. If the mulch is deep enough, it will suppress the growth of many of the weed seeds that may already exist in your soil. Some may be able to break through despite the lack of sunshine, but there is sure to be fewer, and they will be relatively easy to remove.

A well-mulched tree.

REDUCED NEED TO WATER

Watering can be time-consuming and very wasteful.

In my books, any gardening technique that saves water and watering yet keeps your plants well hydrated is worth the effort. Studies have shown that mulching reduces evaporation from the soil by 10 to 50 per cent. Evaporation can be particularly high in hot, dry and windy conditions, but can be a problem in all gardens. Morning dew is not only condensed moisture from the atmosphere that settles on the grass, but also water that has condensed from the air pockets in the soil and been drawn up. Mulch keeps this condensation in the soil, and often absorbs the dew from the atmosphere as well, so there is much less lost to evaporation.

Mulch can also help if too much water or rain is a problem. It will improve poorly draining soil over time, and you can plant directly into some organic mulches rather than in the soil, so your plants don't have wet feet during a rainy spell.

Mulching the root zone of trees is good for them but keep mulch away from the trunks to avoid rot and rodent problems.

Bark chunks look nice, but do not retain moisture like finely ground-up bark.

MODERATED SOIL TEMPERATURE

The "insulating" effect of mulch is often overlooked even by experienced gardeners, yet it can be a real lifesaver for your plants, particularly perennials. A layer of mulch keeps the soil cooler on hot days and warmer on cool days, meaning more gradual shifts in soil temperature.

Roses hilled up and ready for winter.

In the fall and winter, this prevents the soil from freezing quickly and putting plant roots into shock. (Gradual freezing lets roots acclimatize.)

Mulch also minimizes freeze-and-thaw cycles, in which the frozen ground thaws, absorbs moisture from melted snow or rain, and then freezes again in a cold snap. The refrozen earth is now filled with ice crystals, causing the ground to heave, forcing plants out of the soil or exposing roots.

When we "hill up" our roses in the autumn, i.e., mound a 30-centimetre (12-inch) hill of fresh topsoil around the crowns, we are temporarily mulching them to prevent the damage caused by freeze-thaw cycles.

As spring rolls around, moist mulch will delay the warming of the ground. This may sound counterproductive, but it can save plants from coming out of dormancy just as one last late spring freeze hits. In summer, mulch can keep the ground cooler by as much as 6°C (11°F). This is particularly useful in very sunny, hot spots in the garden where high soil temperatures can damage the roots, especially of shallow-rooted or newly planted plants. Alternatively, dark organic mulches and black plastic warm up the soil. In spring, this gives plants a quicker start and, in summer, it will benefit vegetables as well as plants in cool spots in the garden.

LESS COMPACTION AND EROSION

Mulching can control soil erosion, especially on slopes, by slowing runoff during heavy watering or rain. It will also, of course, protect your fine, light topsoil from blowing away in strong winds.

Mulching serves another purpose on rainy days—it cushions the soil, preventing it from being compacted by heavy rain and allowing the water to gently permeate the ground. As the mulch breaks down, it adds organic material to the soil, keeping it friable and "open," and further improving its ability to absorb water.

Aluminum foil as mulch reduces weeds, retains water and reflects the sun for earlier flowering.

REDUCED DISEASE AND INSECT DAMAGE

A layer of mulch can prevent disease spores on the soil from splashing up onto plants during a heavy rainfall and reinfecting them. Dry mulches such as straw placed under vegetables like lettuce and tomatoes prevent rot by keeping the leaves off the moist soil. A deep mulch of straw or leaves (15 centimetres/six inches) can suppress Colorado potato beetles by making it difficult for them to get out from the soil after overwintering.

To combat aphids, I recommend placing a "mulch" of aluminum-coated craft paper (available at the hardware store) or sheets of aluminum foil on the soil around the base of plants. The light shining on the foil confuses winged aphids and makes them lose their sense of direction, so they don't land on the plant. Reducing aphids also reduces the viral diseases that they can spread.

Mulch pulled away from the base of a boxwood shrub.

POTENTIAL PROBLEMS WITH MULCH

Despite my enthusiasm for mulching, I have to admit that the practice has its detractors and there is no doubt that, like any gardening approach, it can have its drawbacks or complications. Here are some potential problems (and solutions) when using mulch.

ANIMALS AND RODENTS

Because mulches act as insulation, small furry creatures can be attracted to this warm blanket in the depths of winter. To prevent mice and other rodents from hiding out and gnawing on the bark of trees and shrubs, keep organic mulch away from the base of the plants. Also, use tightly knit mulches like finely shredded bark mulch and spread it only six to eight centimetres (2 1/2 to three inches) thick. Keep a bottle of rodent repellent (such as Green Earth Animal Repellent, available at most garden centres and hardware stores) on hand to deter them.

A slug heads for the cool dampness of mulch.

Set a slug trap with half a hollowed-out grapefruit.

Slugs will crawl under the grapefruit half and succumb to the acid.

SLUGS AND INSECTS

While earthworms will cheer your yearly application of organic mulch, unfortunately so will slugs. Slugs, as well as a host of other insects both good and bad, like the protection from the sun that mulch provides. If they become a problem, treat them rather than abandoning the benefits of mulch.

There are many ways to depopulate the garden of slugs. Saucers of beer recessed in the ground will attract slugs, which then drown. (I've met people who have tried this method with little effect, to which my answer is: drink the beer yourself and the slug problem won't seem so bad.)

Wood ash and diatomaceous earth around the base of plants also dis-courages slugs and snails. Diatomaceous earth is effective only when dry and must be reapplied if it becomes damp. Overturned grape-fruit halves (with most of their pulp removed) are good traps: slugs crawl under the little dome for protection from the sun only to succumb to the acid from the fruit. And of course, for the unsqueamish, there is always the pick-and-stomp approach.

A wood-chip path.

I do use wood chips as a mulch for many of my paths—particularly tractor paths—but not where people may be walking in bare feet. Wood splinters can be a real hazard.

AIR EXCHANGE

A lack of air exchange through the surface of the soil is only a problem if you mulch too deeply or use plastic mulch. Follow the guidelines listed under "Types of Mulch" (pages 192-199) for correct mulch depths, and move your mulch around occasionally if you notice that it is getting compacted or becoming dense. You may need to remove the plastic or turn it back for a period to improve air exchange. If damping off (a fungal disease that causes young seedlings to collapse) is a problem, keep mulch away from the base of young, tender plants.

Pull leaves away from emerging perennials in early spring.

WATER PENETRATION

Most organic mulches allow water to penetrate well, with the exception of leaves that have matted down. Remove these and put them in your compost bin (shredded leaves are less likely to mat and will decompose faster than whole leaves). Peat moss used as a mulch (which I don't recommend) can form a dry, impermeable crust. It should always be moistened and dug in as a soil amendment, not a mulch.

Inorganic mulches like stone chips and landscape fabrics also allow water to percolate down to the soil. Be sure to use a landscape fabric when laying down stone chips, otherwise you will be forever picking the stones out of your soil. I recommend that you use a professional quality landscape fabric as the difference between it and the consumer brands is significant.

If using plastic mulch, make sure there are generous spaces cut in it around the plants to allow water in.

NITROGEN AVAILABILITY

Perennials, annuals, vegetables and all tender transplants are extremely susceptible to low nitrogen levels, therefore I do not recommend the use of wood chips and sawdust as a mulch in the garden, except on pathways. They may be inexpensive mulches but the downside is that they draw nitrogen from the soil as they decompose. Nitrogen is in greater demand by your garden plants than any other element.

The result of low nitrogen levels in the soil? Yellowing leaves, weaker plants and possible disease and insect infestation.

Lava rock allows water penetration.

Cedar bark mulch gives perennials a cool, moist root run.

ADDING SOIL AMENDMENTS

Some people are reluctant to mulch their flower beds because they think it will make it difficult to amend the soil afterward. But if you are using organic mulches, they are amending your soil as they break down.

In the spring and fall, when you want to add compost to your soil, rake aside the mulch, add the compost or fallen leaves to your soil and then replace the mulch. Don't worry if you don't get all the mulch—organic mulches can be dug into the soil with the compost.

Easier still, you can leave organic mulch in place and apply new soil or amendments on top of it every two or three years.

When you add a new plant to the garden, rake aside the mulch, dig the hole, add the compost or triple mix, do your planting and then replace the mulch. It is a little bit more time-consuming, but experience has taught me that it's very much worth it.

Snow is an excellent insulator.

WINTER / SUMMER MULCHES

WINTER MULCH

This is applied after the first hard frost to prevent the damage of freeze/thaw cycles that can heave plants, especially woody ones, out of the soil. Don't apply winter mulch too early or the ground will stay warm and plants won't go into necessary dormancy. In addition to good mulches like chopped leaves, straw, bark, etc., snow can act as an effective winter mulch. Shovel dry snow (making sure it isn't contaminated with road salt) onto your flower beds for added insulation.

Chopped leaves as mulch.

The following spring, use a rake or fine hoe to carefully scrape the mulch from around the plants and spread it over the beds. Add more mulch if necessary.

SUMMER MULCH

This is applied after the soil has warmed to 18°C (64°F) to get all the benefits outlined at the start of this chapter (see page 185). Before mulching, weed thoroughly and water the soil if it's dry. Be sure to use the recommended depth of mulch (see "Types of Mulch," in the following pages). Too little mulch won't inhibit weeds or prevent evaporation as effectively. Too much can hinder water penetration, restrict air circulation and smother tiny seedlings.

Keep organic mulch approximately 15 centimetres (six inches) away from the trunks of trees, the base of shrubs and the crowns of perennials. Mounding mulch too close can lead to rot and potential damage from rodents or insects.

Bark chunks.

Shredded bark.

TYPES OF MULCH - ORGANIC

There are many mulching materials, both organic and inorganic, for different applications, so check the list below to choose the right one for your needs.

BARK

Unless you have a woodlot or know someone who does, you will likely be purchasing this in a garden centre or landscape supply company. There are a host of bark mulches on the market and their quality varies enormously. A good bark mulch should contain no more than 10 percent wood chips, and should not have any significant quantity of dirt or sand. Be cautious of anything that does not say "bark" on the packaging: some mulches labelled "red mulch" are primarily red-coloured wood chunks rather than bark.

A quality bark mulch may be a tad more expensive but it can be very attractive and you'll probably find it

well worth the few extra dollars. Here are some interesting points about bark mulch:

- Bark doesn't include the heartwood of the tree.

- Bark decomposes slowly (it can take up to four years, although some shredded barks may break down more quickly).

- Redwoods are rot-resistant so they are not as good a source of humus as some other barks.

- Earthworms do not seem to favour redwood products.

- Pine decomposes quickly.

BARK CHUNKS AND CHIPS

Apply chunks to a depth of two to eight centimetres (3/4 to three inches) and chips four to six centimetres (1 1/2 to 2 1/2 inches) deep. Use them around

well-established trees and shrubs. Be aware that chunks and chips may wash away on slopes or get moved off beds.

SHREDDED OR FIBRE BARK

Apply six to eight centimetres (two to three inches) deep.

This is my favourite type of mulch because it knits together when dry; isn't washed or blown away; and smothers weeds. I use a high-quality finely ground red cedar bark—an attractive, fragrant mulch that comes out of the bag damp. Once spread, the fibres knit together, forming a blanket that stays in place but still allows water to percolate through.

After two to four years, it will begin to break down, adding valuable organic matter to the soil. At this time, you simply spread another layer six to eight centimetres (two to three inches) deep over the bed.

Cocoa hulls.

Coffee grounds.

Compost piles at Kew Gardens, England. A tourist attraction!

COCOA HULLS

Apply four to five centimetres (1 1/2 to two inches) deep. Cocoa hulls often give off the aroma of chocolate, especially when wet, and their dark colour is reminiscent of the candy. Some people like this and others find it a bit off-putting, but either way the odour is short-lived (it disappears in two or three weeks).

The dark hulls absorb heat and warm up the soil rapidly. They don't tie up nitrogen but decompose quickly (over one to two seasons depending on contact with water), adding nutrients to the soil. This rapid breakdown means they need replacing more often than some other mulches.

On the downside, they can wash away on inclines or blow away in a stiff wind and they retain moisture so can get slimy or develop moulds. This is unsightly but not harmful and can be resolved by turning the mouldy layer under. I move my cocoa mulch around with a hoe or cultivator every few weeks to help minimize mould build-up.

Also, avoid using cocoa hulls if you have pet dogs—the smell can be tempting, and chocolate in any form can be toxic to them if eaten. Based on personal experience, this is a very real possi-bility. Our dog has certainly munched on the stuff and been ill but thankfully has lived to munch again.

COFFEE GROUNDS

While some people like to use coffee grounds as a light (2.5-centimetre/one-inch) mulch—you may know garden-ers who sprinkle them around their roses or rhododendrons—my experi-ence is that they are best added to your compost bin or dug into the soil, where they will add some acidity. As a mulch, they can compact and dry out, hamper-ing water penetration. Some coffee shops will give their grounds away to homeowners (it is a corporate policy of Starbucks); others give them only to municipal composting or community garden groups.

EVERGREEN BOUGHS

If you have boughs from pruning your evergreens or from your Christmas tree and seasonal decorating, don't throw them out. They can be beautiful and useful as a winter mulch laid over newly planted or fragile perennials. Snow will collect on top as insulation but the branches will prevent the weight of ice and snow from damaging the plants. Carefully placed boughs can also protect heathers, azaleas and rho-dodendrons from burning in the winter sun.

COMPOST

Apply two to five centimetres (3/4 to two inches) deep. Most people tend to think of compost as a soil amend-ment that works nicely under other mulches, but partly decomposed compost can be used as a mulch itself. It will work its way into the soil (thanks to your earthworms), improving both the nutrient content and composition of your soil. As a mulch, it is less effective at weed reduction and moisture retention. Given that good compost is hard to come by—backyard composters never seem to make enough—and well-rotted manure can be expensive, I recommend that you keep these for soil amendment and add a different organic mulch on top.

Evergreen boughs.

Japanese spurge (Pachysandra) is a reliable groundcover to zone 5.

While not generally listed under mulches in most books, groundcovers do serve many of the same functions. They keep soil covered to prevent soil erosion and moisture loss, reduce weeds, moderate temperatures and look attractive, especially under trees and shrubs. Some can stand some foot traffic, too. A small industry has sprung up around the concept of "living mulches" in recent years.

Check out www.stepables.com and www.jeeperscreepers.info for more information.

Grass clippings.

Clover cover crop.

GRASS CLIPPINGS

Apply to the surface of the soil no deeper than four to five centimetres (1 1/2 to two inches). As long as your grass is not extremely long when you cut it, clippings are best left on the lawn. This raw organic material will rot down into the soil, adding nitrogen as it goes. But if you have a lot of clippings and your lawn hasn't been treated with herbicide (See Chapter 12 for more on organic lawn care), you can use them as a mulch. Grass clippings can get slimy (and smelly) quite rapidly so let them dry before piling them around plants. They will decompose quickly (drawing nitrogen from the soil in the process), so won't last long. I find that they work best as a mulch around vegetables or used to reduce weeds on paths in your vegetable garden.

GREEN MULCHES

Green mulches, also known as green manure, are often used in vegetable gardening. They are cover crops such as ryegrass, winter barley or white clover that are sown after the harvest is finished and left in the ground over winter. They act like a green coat for the soil, preventing erosion from water and wind, and suppressing weed growth.

In spring, they are ploughed under, giving the soil a boost of nitrogen and other nutrients. Legumes are especially valuable as they fix nitrogen in the soil even before they are dug under.

In quantity, large leaves like these maple leaves can mat down, stopping weed penetration.

Chopped leaves as a mulch let air and water through.

Oak leaves should be shredded for quicker decomposition.

LEAVES

Apply 10 to 15 centimetres (four to six inches) deep. Many garden experts decry the common habit of raking leaves and then bagging them for the garbage. Personally, I rather like it when my neighbours do this as I get to steal the bags from the end of their driveway.

I spread leaves as a winter mulch around most of my perennials. This insulates the soil and eliminates weeding early in spring. Every fall, I also spread a layer of leaves five to seven centimetres (two to 2 1/2 inches) deep over my entire vegetable garden. Come spring, I rototill them under, adding valuable organic content to the soil. My veggies thank me with fantastic growth!

Leaves are a terrific mulch; they are free and readily available; they provide carbon, a much-needed ingredient in all successful soil types; and offer all the other benefits of a good mulch (See Benefits of Mulch, page185).

Large leaves such as maple and catalpa can form thick mats, keeping water and air from the soil, and some leaves such as oak and beech take a long time to break down. Chopping your leaves into small pieces speeds decomposition and increases air circulation to the soil. The mulch is also less likely to blow away.

To chop leaves, run them through a shredder if you have one, or run over them with a lawn mower. A power mower with a grass catcher makes this task easier, as you can collect the shredded leaves as you go. Make sure that your mower is set at its highest setting, and keep in mind that dry leaves shred more easily. I fill large kraft paper leaf bags with leaves, stomp on them to compact them in the bag and stack the bags like cordwood against a shed at the back of the yard. Come spring, the leaves are semi-decomposed and ready to be used as a valuable mulch.

Pine needle mulch.

NEWSPRINT
Apply two to four centimetres (3/4 to 1 1/2 inches) deep, unshredded; four to eight centimetres (1 1/2 to three inches) deep, shredded. Newspapers are often used on vegetable beds, but they can also be used on flower beds and top-dressed with another organic mulch (they're not very attractive on their own). You can shred the paper, tear it into strips or lay it in sheets. Make sure you wet both the soil and the newspapers before laying them down permanently and water thoroughly afterward so they won't blow away.

Newsprint is inexpensive and readily available, and mulching is an excellent way to recycle it. All newspapers now use vegetable dye inks, so they are safe for use in the garden.

PINE NEEDLES
Apply eight to 15 centimetres (three to six inches) deep. If you have a lot of pine trees on your property or have a cottage, these won't be hard to collect. Pine needle mulch smells and looks attractive and won't wash away on slopes.

The needles can be worked into the soil if you want extra acidity, although they are slow to decompose so it will take two or three years to have a significant effect on soil pH. They make an excellent mulch for rhododendrons, azaleas and boxwood. Pine needles may control fungal diseases to some extent, but discourage earthworms. I have also seen pine and spruce cones used as a decorative mulch to great effect!

Pine cones used as a decorative mulch.

SAWDUST

I don't recommend using sawdust as a mulch. Not only does it leach nitrogen from the soil initially, it tends to overheat (a fire hazard!) and looks unappealing. If you have sawdust, better to compost it with generous layers of leaves and grass clippings.

Wood chips.

Dyed red wood chips.

Black wood chips.

WOOD CHIPS

Apply eight to 10 centimetres (three to four inches) deep. Wood chips obtained from retailers and sold specifically as a mulch do not come from pressure-treated wood, but if you've collected them from a tree removal expert or from a sawmill, make sure they are untreated, as chemicals can leach from treated wood into the soil.

Also, remember that the thinner the wood chips or shavings, the more nitrogen they will absorb from the soil. Soft woods (pine, cedar, spruce) absorb far more nitrogen from the soil than do hardwoods, so use wood chips only under and around well-established plants, shrubs and trees or on a garden path.

Wood chips lose their colour faster than bark chips and may look unattractive after a while. Organically dyed wood chips in shades of red, brown and even blue are now available. They can be attractive accents for the garden but they have the same nitrogen consumption as the undyed wood.

If you buy wood chips (either packaged or from a sawmill) and you notice an odour of rotten eggs, ammonia or vinegar, don't use them. The chips have gone "sour" or anaerobic (that is, decomposing without sufficient oxygen) and are producing substances such as methanol, acetic acid and ammonia that will harm the plants. Spread the chips out and let them dry. Turn them regularly to let the air get at them before using.

STRAW (NOT HAY!)

Apply 15 to 20 centimetres (six to eight inches) deep. Straw is ideal for the vegetable garden, especially tomatoes, peppers and potatoes—it keeps leaves dry and away from damp soil. It's also the best mulch for strawberries (which is how they got their name). On a bed of straw the fruit is kept clean and bug-free.

I find it unattractive on flower beds, but as it is so inexpensive and readily available (garden centres carry it), you may want to use it anyway. Simply camouflage it with a couple of centimetres (an inch) of a better-looking mulch.

Make sure that your straw is seed-free before using. It will draw nitrogen from the soil during decomposition so amend with lots of compost before mulching.

TYPES OF MULCH - INORGANIC

Inorganic mulches refer to those not derived from living things.

BLACK PLASTIC

While not particularly attractive, black plastic can be very useful as a vegetable garden mulch. It is being used extensively on commercial farms.

Prepare the soil and lay sheets of plastic over the rows, anchoring the edges with soil or rocks. Make X-shaped slits where you want to plant the seedlings. Alternatively, you can lay strips of plastic between the rows.

Black plastic warms the soil: use it for heat-loving vegetables such as tomatoes, peppers, cucumbers, squash, corn and eggplant. It also prevents weed seeds in the soil from germinating and airborne seeds from taking root, and limits evaporation from the soil. On the downside, water can't penetrate unless the plastic is slit or punctured, and it does inhibit air circulation so check plants for crown rot or damping off. It also usually lasts only one season.

CLEAR PLASTIC

Clear plastic can be used in the same way as black plastic. Since it allows the sun to penetrate, it can warm up the soil even faster (at least initially), giving plants an early start. This is a bonus in northern climates. Like black plastic, it prevents evaporation and weed growth, but must be punctured to admit water. It also inhibits air circulation and usually lasts one season. Weeds can grow under it in mild weather, but they will be killed by the heat once hot weather arrives.

Tumbled gravel needs heavy landscape fabric under it to prevent weeds and stop the gravel from migrating into the soil.

GEOTEXTILES (LANDSCAPE FABRIC)

Geotextiles (from *geo* meaning "earth") are permeable synthetic materials used with soil and rock. Landscape fabric is one of the most popular and useful of these textiles. It allows air and water to pass through, but blocks the light that weed seeds need to germinate and grow. The fabric needs to be top-dressed with a centimetre (3/8 inch) or so of another mulch to make it more attractive and prevent it from deteriorating in the sunlight. More permanent than organic mulch, covered landscape fabric can last over five years.

Black landscape fabric.

Fabric can be difficult to move to amend the soil or plant annuals and vegetables so you may want to use it only around more fixed plantings such as trees or shrubs. Geotextiles are also effective at preventing soil erosion, especially on slopes.

GRAVEL

Gravel or aggregates can be useful mulches from an esthetic point of view; they allow water through and keep the soil cool. As time passes, they tend to look weather-worn. The real downside to their use is that they inevitably become incorporated into the soil beneath them. When this happens, watch out! They are a downright nuisance and you'll risk broken fingernails every time you move your hands through the soil.

Putting down a double layer of landscape fabric before spreading the gravel will avoid a lot of these problems—for some years, anyway!

PLANT HARDINESS ZONE MAP OF CANADA

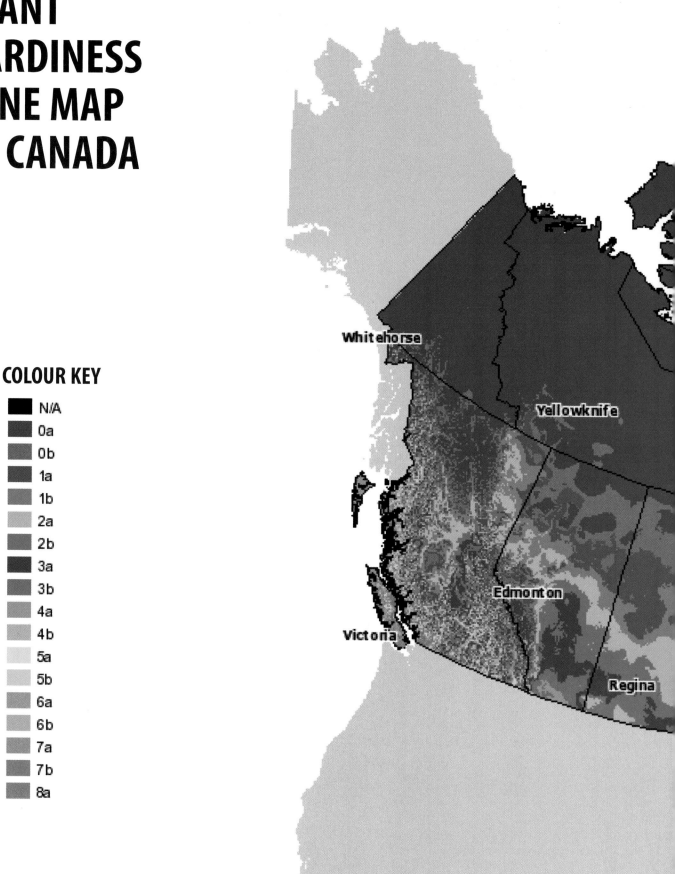

COLOUR KEY

- N/A
- 0a
- 0b
- 1a
- 1b
- 2a
- 2b
- 3a
- 3b
- 4a
- 4b
- 5a
- 5b
- 6a
- 6b
- 7a
- 7b
- 8a

Whitehorse

Yellowknife

Edmonton

Victoria

Regina

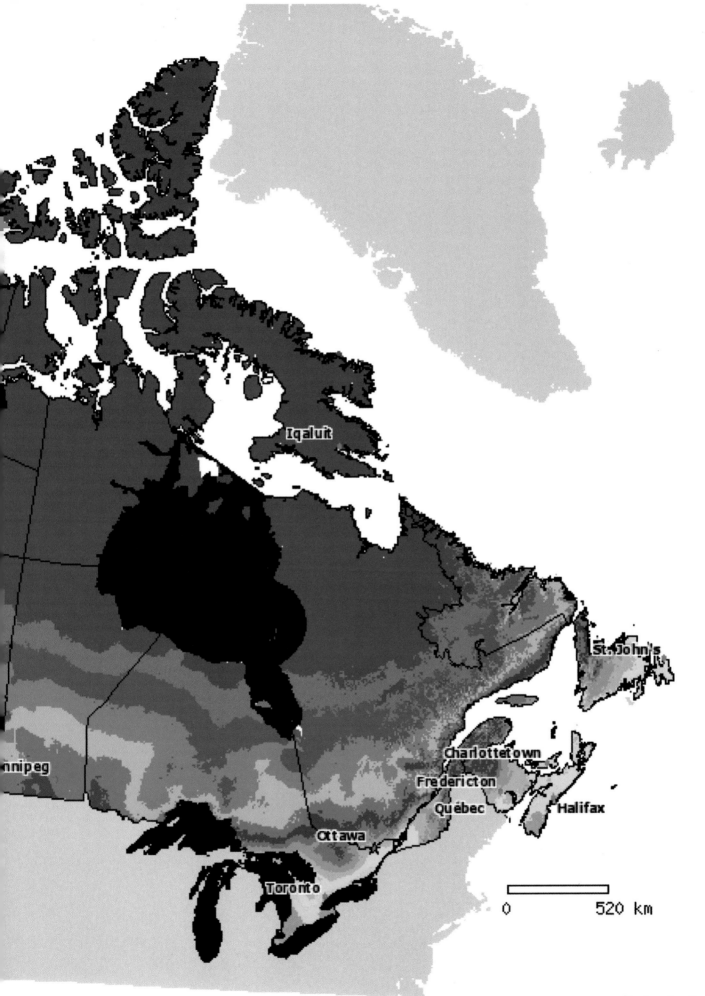

Hardiness Zone Map 201

INDEX

Note: Page numbers in italics refer to photographs

PHOTO CREDITS

© 2008 Frances Juriansz   Cover photograph

Vincenzo Pietropaolo   Author photograph and back cover
photograph

Emma Cullen   18 *right*, 28 *bottom left*, 29 *top*, 31 *top right*,

49 *top right*, 67 *mid right*,

100 *bottom middle*, 147 *top and bottom left*,

149, 150, 160 *left*, 162, 163

Mark Cullen   12 *bottom right*, 13 *bottom right*,

14 *bottom left*, 15 *right*, 16, 17 *bottom left*,

18 *bottom left*, 21 *bottom*, 22, 23 *top*,

26 *top left and bottom right*, 27, 28 *top*,

38 *top left*, 41 *top right*, 42, 45 *mid right*,

46 *top left*, 49 *top left and bottom left*,

55 *top right*, 61 *bottom left*, 63 *bottom*,

67 *top*, 68 *mid right*, 70, 74 *top left*, 78,

92 *mid right*, 94 *mid right*,

96, 99, 113 *top*, 115 *top left*,

128, 129, 135 *top*, 137 *top left*,

146, 152, 155 *bottom left*,

169 *top right*, 170, 171, 173 *top*,

178 *bottom*,185 *top left*, 193 *top right*,

194 *mid right*, 196 *bottom*

Andrew Graham   6 *top right*

Brenda Hensley	6 *top left*, 7, *top left and right*, 8, 10, 11, 12 *top left*, 13 *bottom left*, 14 *top*, 15 *left*, 17 *bottom right*, 18 *top left*, 19, 20, 21 *top right*, 23 *bottom left*, 24, 25, 26 *bottom left*, 29 *bottom left*, 30 *bottom right*, 32, 33, 34 *top left*, 35 *top right*, 36 *top*, 37, 38 *top right*, *mid-right, bottom left and bottom right*, 39, 40, 41 *bottom*, 43, 44, 45 *top right and bottom left & right*, 46 *mid right and bottom*, 47, 50-54, 55 *bottom left*, 56-60, 61 *top*, 62, 63 *top and mid-right*, 64-66, 68 *top left and mid left*, 69, 71-77, 80-91, 92 *top left*, 93, 94 *top left and middle*, 95, 97, 100 *bottom middle*, 102-104, 106-114, 115 *bottom left and mid right*, 116-126, 130-134, 135 *bottom left*, 136, 137 *mid right*, 138-145, 147 *right*, 148, 153, 154, 155 *top*, 156, 157-159, 160 *right*, 161, 164-168, 169 *bottom left*, 172, 173 *bottom left*, 174-177, 178 *top*, 179-184, 185 *top right*, 186-192, 193 *top left, top middle and bottom right*, 194 *top left and mid left*, 195, 196 *top*, 197-199
Christopher Laird	79 *bottom right*, 98, 100 *top and bottom right*
Larry Parr	151
Pathways to Perennials *www.pathwaystoperrenials.com*	34 *bottom*, 35 *top left*
Alexandra Stephanson	*inside front flap*
Denise Thomson *markcullen.com contest winner*	30 *top left*, 31 *bottom right*